C000140784

AAT

Business Tax FA 2016

Level 4

Professional Diploma in Accounting

Question Bank

For assessments up to August 2018

Second edition 2016

ISBN 9781 5097 1503 9

British Library Cataloguing-in-Publication Data
A catalogue record for this book is available from the British Library

Published by

BPP Learning Media Ltd
BPP House, Aldine Place
142-144 Uxbridge Road
London W12 8AA

www.bpp.com/learningmedia

Printed in the United Kingdom

Your learning materials, published by BPP Learning Media Ltd, are printed on paper obtained from traceable sustainable sources.

We are grateful to the AAT for permission to reproduce the sample assessment(s). The answers to the sample assessment(s) have been published by the AAT. All other answers have been prepared by BPP Learning Media Ltd.

Contents

Introduction

This is BPP Learning Media's AAT Question Bank for *Business Tax*. It is part of a suite of ground-breaking resources produced by BPP Learning Media for AAT assessments.

This Question Bank has been written in conjunction with the BPP Course Book, and has been carefully designed to enable students to practise all of the learning outcomes and assessment criteria for the units that make up *Business Tax*. It is fully up to date as at June 2016 and reflects both the AAT's qualification specification and the sample assessment provided by the AAT.

This Question Bank contains these key features:

- Tasks corresponding to each chapter of the Course Book. Some tasks are designed for learning purposes, others are of assessment standard
- AAT's AQ2016 sample assessment 1 and answers for *Business Tax* and further BPP practice assessments. (The AAT sample assessment included in the Question Bank is a draft version. The AAT reserves the right to change the material.)

The emphasis in all tasks and assessments is on the practical application of the skills acquired.

Assessment up to 31 August 2018 will use the rules contained in Finance Act 2016 so tasks will focus on tax rates and thresholds for the tax year 2016/17 and financial year 2016. It may be that you have to deal with other tax years at work, in which case the rates and thresholds you use will be different. This Question Bank is focused on your assessment up to 31 August 2018.

VAT

You may find tasks throughout this Question Bank that need you to calculate or be aware of a rate of VAT. This is stated at 20% in these examples and questions. (The AAT sample assessment included in the Question Bank is a draft version. The AAT reserves the right to change the material.)

Approaching the assessment

When you sit the assessment it is very important that you follow the on screen instructions. This means you need to carefully read the instructions, both on the introduction screens and during specific tasks.

When you access the assessment you should be presented with an introductory screen with information similar to that shown below (taken from the introductory screen from one of the AAT's AQ2016 sample assessments for *Business Tax*).

> We have provided this **sample assessment** to help you familiarise yourself with our e-assessment environment. It is designed to demonstrate as many of the question types that you may find in a live assessment as possible. It is not designed to be used on its own to determine whether you are ready for a live assessment.
>
> At the end of this sample assessment you will receive an immediate result. This will **not** take into account your response to tasks 3, 4, 9 and 11. In the live assessment these tasks will be human marked so you will not receive an immediate result.

Assessment information:

You have **2 hours** to complete this sample assessment.

This assessment contains **11 tasks** and you should attempt to complete every task.
Each task is independent. You will not need to refer to your answers in previous tasks.
Read every task carefully to make sure you understand what is required.

Task 9 requires extended writing as part of your response to the questions. You should make sure you allow adequate time to complete this task.

Where the date is relevant, it is given in the task data.

You may use minus signs or brackets to indicate negative numbers **unless** task instructions say otherwise.

You must use a full stop to indicate a decimal point.
For example, write 100.57 NOT 100,57 or 100 57

You may use a comma to indicate a number in the thousands, but you don't have to.
For example, 10000 and 10,000 are both acceptable.

If rounding is required, normal mathematical rounding rules should be applied **unless** task instructions say otherwise.

The actual instructions will vary depending on the subject you are studying for. It is very important you read the instructions on the introductory screen and apply them in the assessment. You don't want to lose marks when you know the correct answer just because you have not entered it in the right format.

In general, the rules set out in the AAT sample assessments for the subject you are studying for will apply in the real assessment, but you should carefully read the information on this screen again in the real assessment, just to make sure. This screen may also confirm the VAT rate used if applicable.

A full stop is needed to indicate a decimal point. We would recommend using minus signs to indicate negative numbers and leaving out the comma signs to indicate thousands, as this results in a lower number of key strokes and less margin for error when working under time pressure. Having said that, you can use whatever is easiest for you as long as you operate within the rules set out for your particular assessment.

You have to show competence throughout the assessment and you should therefore complete all of the tasks. Don't leave questions unanswered.

In some assessments, written or complex tasks may be human marked. In this case you are given a blank space or table to enter your answer into. You are told in the assessments which tasks these are (**Note.** There may be none if all answers are marked by the computer).

If these involve calculations, it is a good idea to decide in advance how you are going to lay out your answers to such tasks by practising answering them on a word document, and certainly you should try all such tasks in this Question Bank and in the AAT's environment using the sample assessment.

When asked to fill in tables, or gaps, never leave any blank even if you are unsure of the answer. Fill in your best estimate.

Note that for some assessments where there is a lot of scenario information or tables of data provided (eg tax tables), you may need to access these via 'pop-ups'. Instructions will be provided on how you can bring up the necessary data during the assessment.

Finally, take note of any task specific instructions once you are in the assessment. For example you may be asked to enter a date in a certain format or to enter a number to a certain number of decimal places.

Grading

To achieve the qualification and to be awarded a grade, you must pass all the mandatory unit assessments, all optional unit assessments (where applicable) and the synoptic assessment.

The AAT Level 4 Professional Diploma in Accounting will be awarded a grade. This grade will be based on performance across the qualification. Unit assessments and synoptic assessments are not individually graded. These assessments are given a mark that is used in calculating the overall grade.

How overall grade is determined

You will be awarded an overall qualification grade (Distinction, Merit, and Pass). If you do not achieve the qualification you will not receive a qualification certificate, and the grade will be shown as unclassified.

The marks of each assessment will be converted into a percentage mark and rounded up or down to the nearest whole number. This percentage mark is then weighted according to the weighting of the unit assessment or synoptic assessment within the qualification. The resulting weighted assessment percentages are combined to arrive at a percentage mark for the whole qualification.

Grade definition	Percentage threshold
Distinction	90–100%
Merit	80–89%
Pass	70–79%
Unclassified	0–69% Or failure to pass one or more assessment/s

Re-sits

The AAT Professional Diploma In Accounting is not subject to re-sit restrictions.

You should only be entered for an assessment when you are well prepared and you expect to pass the assessment.

AAT qualifications

The material in this book may support the following AAT qualifications:

AAT Professional Diploma in Accounting Level 4, AAT Professional Diploma in Accounting at SCQF Level 8 and Certificate: Accounting (Level 5 AATSA).

Supplements

From time to time we may need to publish supplementary materials to one of our titles. This can be for a variety of reasons. From a small change in the AAT unit guidance to new legislation coming into effect between editions.

You should check our supplements page regularly for anything that may affect your learning materials. All supplements are available free of charge on our supplements page on our website at:

www.bpp.com/learning-media/about/students

Improving material and removing errors

There is a constant need to update and enhance our study materials in line with both regulatory changes and new insights into the assessments.

From our team of authors BPP appoints a subject expert to update and improve these materials for each new edition.

Their updated draft is subsequently technically checked by another author and from time to time non-technically checked by a proof reader.

We are very keen to remove as many numerical errors and narrative typos as we can but given the volume of detailed information being changed in a short space of time we know that a few errors will sometimes get through our net.

We apologise in advance for any inconvenience that an error might cause. We continue to look for new ways to improve these study materials and would welcome your suggestions. If you have any comments about this book, please email nisarahmed@bpp.com or write to Nisar Ahmed, AAT Head of Programme, BPP Learning Media Ltd, BPP House, Aldine Place, London W12 8A.

Question Bank

Chapter 1 Tax framework

Task 1.1

Listed below are 3 different methods of operating a business.

Put a tick in the relevant column to say whether the business method is incorporated or unincorporated.

	Incorporated ✓	Unincorporated ✓
Sole trader		✓
Partnership		✓
Limited company	✓	

Task 1.2

The profits generated by different business methods suffer different taxes.

Show which taxes are suffered by profits generated by each business method by linking the following business methods to the appropriate taxes in the right-hand boxes.

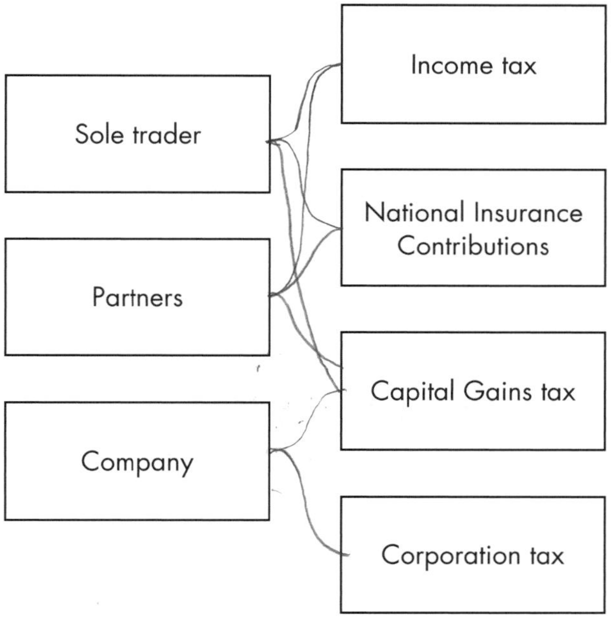

Task 1.3

Listed below are several sources of tax law and practice.

Put a tick in the relevant column to say whether the source has the force of law or not.

	Force of law ✓	No force of law ✓
Statute law	✓	
Act of Parliament	✓	
Statutory Instrument	✓	
HMRC guidance		✓
Case Law	✓	

Task 1.4

Which of the following actions by a taxpayer would not constitute tax evasion?

	✓
Claiming capital allowances on a fictitious piece of equipment	
Failing to notify HMRC of a profitable trade commenced three years ago	
Obtaining tax-free interest by investing in an ISA	✓
Deciding not to declare rental income received	

Task 1.5

List TWO ethical duties and responsibilities of an accountant.

Confidentiality – keeping client information private

Integrity – being honest & truthful

Task 1.6

Tax avoidance ▼ is the use of loopholes in tax legislation to minimise tax liabilities.

Tax planning ▼ is the use of all available reliefs in the manner intended to minimise tax liabilities.

Tax evasion ▼ is the deliberate misleading of tax authorities to minimise tax liabilities.

Picklist:

avoidance
evasion
planning

Chapter 2 Computing trading income

Task 2.1

When deciding whether a trade is being carried on, HM Revenue and Customs is often guided by the badges of trade.

Write a memo to a client who is concerned they may be trading, explaining what is meant by the term badges of trade.

From: AAT student
To: A Client
Date: 14 June
Subject: Badges of trade

The badges of trade are what HMRC use to decide if an individual is trading

Subject matter - is it normal to purchase what you have

Ownership - how long did you own the goods before selling. Shorter indicates trade

Frequency of transactions - how often is this occurring. More often indicates trade

Improvement expenditure - have you done anything to the product before selling

Reason for sale - why are you selling

motive for profit - are you doing it to intentionally make a profit

This page is for the continuation of your memo. You may not need all of it.

Task 2.2

Decide how each of the following items would be treated in the tax computation of a sole trader. Tick ONE box per line.

	Allow ✓	Disallow and add back ✓	Not taxable so deduct ✓
Gifts of 30 bottles of wine to clients		✓	
Lease costs of a car with emissions of 150g/km		✓ (15%)	
Costs of £5,000 to repair a roof	✓		
£1,000 cost to register a patent	✓		
Accounting profit on disposal of a van			✓
£500 donation to a political party		✓	
Repair to factory roof	✓		

Task 2.3

The statement of profit or loss for Mr Jelly for the year ended 31 December shows:

	£		£
Staff wages	12,500	Gross profit from trading account	20,000
Light and heat	162		
Motor car expenses	350		
Postage, stationery and telephone	100		
Repairs and renewals	450		
Irrecoverable debts	238		
Miscellaneous expenses	300		

	£		£
Depreciation charge	600		
Profit for the year	5,300		
	20,000		20,000

The following information is also relevant:

(1) The staff wages include £260 paid to Mr Jelly.
(2) One-seventh of the motor expenses relates to private motoring.
(3) Repairs and renewals comprise:

	£
Painting shop internally	129
Plant repairs	220
Building extension to stockroom	101
	450

(4) **Irrecoverable debt provisions**

		£			£
			Jan 1	Balances b/f	
Dec 31	Balances c/f			General	200
	General	400		Specific	360
	Specific	398			
			Dec 31	Statement of profit or loss	238
		798			798

(5) **Miscellaneous expenses include:**

	£
Donations – Oxfam	10
Advertising	115
Customer entertaining	90
Christmas gifts – ten bottles of gin and whisky	70
Legal expenses re debt collecting	15
	300

Using the proforma layout provided, compute Mr Jelly's taxable trading profit for the year ended 31 December. Input 0 (zero) if necessary, in order to fill in all unshaded boxes.

	£	£
Profit for the year per accounts		5300
	Add	Deduct
Staff wages	0	0
Mr Jelly's salary	260	0
Light and heat	0	0
Motor expenses	50	0
Postage, stationery and telephone	0	0
Painting shop internally	0	0
Plant repairs	0	0
Stockroom extension	101	0
Provision	200	0
Donations	10	0
Advertising	0	0
Entertaining	90	0
Gifts	70	0
Legal expenses	0	0

	£	£
Depreciation charge	600	0
Total net adjustments		1381
Taxable trading profit		6681

Task 2.4

Decide how each of the following items would be treated in the tax computation of a sole trader. Tick ONE box per line.

	Allow ✓	Disallow and add back ✓	Not taxable so deduct ✓
Increase in specific provision	✓		
Decrease in general provision			✓
Depreciation charge		✓	
Cocktail party held for customers		✓	
Political donation		✓	
Employees salary	✓		
Repair to factory roof	✓		

Task 2.5

Graham has carried on business for many years making up accounts to 31 March each year.

The following information is relevant to his period of account to 31 March 2017:

	£
Revenue	150,000
Cost of goods bought	25,000
Heating	1,200
Insurance	560
Office costs	1,700
Bank charges	150
Accountancy and legal costs (£500 disallowable as relates to capital)	1,650
Goods taken for own use (market value)	750
New car (CO_2 emissions 170 g/km)	19,000

Using this information, complete the self-employment page below.

Business expenses

Please read the *Self-employment (full) notes* before filling in this section.

Box	Total expenses	£	Box	Disallowable expenses	£
	If your annual turnover was below £83,000 you may just put your total expenses in box 31			Use this column if the figures in boxes 17 to 30 include disallowable amounts	
17	Cost of goods bought for resale or goods used	25000.00	32		[illegible].00
18	Construction industry – *payments to subcontractors*	.00	33		.00
19	Wages, salaries and other staff costs	.00	34		.00
20	Car, van and travel expenses	.00	35		.00
21	Rent, rates, power and insurance costs	1760.00	36		.00
22	Repairs and renewals of property and equipment	.00	37		.00
23	Phone, fax, stationery and other office costs	1700.00	38		.00
24	Advertising and business entertainment costs	.00	39		.00
25	Interest on bank and other loans	.00	40		.00
26	Bank, credit card and other financial charges	150.00	41		.00
27	Irrecoverable debts written off	.00	42		.00
28	Accountancy, legal and other professional fees	1650.00	43		500.00
29	Depreciation and loss/profit on sale of assets	.00	44		.00
30	Other business expenses	.00	45		.00
31	Total expenses (total of boxes 17 to 30)	30260.00	46	Total disallowable expenses (total of boxes 32 to 45)	500.00

SA103F 2016 Page SEF 2

(Adapted from HMRC, 2016)

Chapter 3 Capital allowances

Task 3.1

For the following items of expenditure, tick if they are revenue or capital:

	Revenue ✓	Capital ✓
Purchase of machinery		✓
Rent paid for premises	✓	
Insurance of premises	✓	
Repairs to roof of factory	✓	
New extension to shop		✓
Purchase of new car for owner		✓
Legal fees relating to purchase of new factory		✓
Payment of staff wages	✓	
Accountancy costs	✓	
Redecoration of shop	✓	

Task 3.2

Bodie, a sole trader, makes up his accounts to 30 June each year. The value of the main pool as at 1 July 2015 was £38,500.

His expenditure, all qualifying for capital allowances, has been as follows:

Date		£
14 January 2016	Office furniture	23,800
30 March 2016	Mercedes car – CO_2 emissions 120g/km	18,000
31 March 2016	Car – CO_2 emissions 100g/km	8,000
2 June 2016	Machinery	31,000

The Mercedes was for the proprietor's own use (20% private), while the other car was for an employee.

Machinery which had been acquired for £7,000 was sold for £3,000 on 29 March 2016.

Using the proforma layout provided, calculate capital allowances for the year ending 30 June 2016.

	Main	AIA	Car	
WDV b/fwd	38500	0	0	
Addition Office	~~23800~~	23800		
Merc			18000	
Car	8000			
Machinery		31000		
Disposal Machinery	(3000)			
	43500	54800	18000	
AIA		(54800)		
WDA @18%	(7830)		(3240)	
WDV c/fwd	35670	0	14760	
	WDA	Private use	B/U	
WDA to charge for Merc	3240	(648)	2592	
AIA	54800			
WDA	7830			
Merc	2592			
Capital Allowances for year	65222			

Task 3.3

Wolfgang commences to trade on 1 April 2016. During his first year, he incurs the following expenditure:

		£
6 May 2016	Machinery	218,250
6 July 2016	Car with CO_2 emissions of 70g/km	8,000
31 August 2016	Car with CO_2 emissions of 125g/km	10,500

Using the proforma layout provided, compute the capital allowance available to Wolfgang for the year ended 31 March 2017.

	Main	AIA	FYA	
WDV b/fwd	0	0	0	
Additions Machinery	18250	200000		
Car 70g/km			8000	
Car 125g/km	10500			
	28750	200000	8000	
AIA		(200000)		
FYA			(8000)	
WDA 18%	(5175)			
WDV c/fwd	23575	0	0	
AIA	200000			
FYA	8000			
WDA	5175			
Capital allowance	213175			

Task 3.4

Rachel is a sole trader making up accounts to 31 March each year.

On 1 October 2015, the brought forward balances on her plant and machinery were as follows:

	£
Main pool	120,000
Car – private use 30% by Rachel	21,000
Special rate pool	17,500

She sold the car she used privately for £16,000 on 10 August 2016 and bought another car (CO_2 emissions 170g/km) on the same day for £25,000, which also had 30% private use by her.

Using the proforma layout provided, calculate the capital allowances available in the year to 30 September 2016.

	Main	~~AIA~~ Private use	Private use special	Special	
WDV b/fwd	120000	21000	~~[illegible]~~	17500	
Addition			25000		
Disposal		(16000)			
	120000	5000	25000	17500	
Balancing charge		(5000)			
	120000	0	25000	17500	
WDA 18%	(21600)				
WDA 8%			(2000)	(1400)	
	98400	0	23000	16100	
	WDA	PU	BU		
Private use	2000	(600)	1400	Balancing	5000
				WDA	21600
				Private use	1400
				Special	1400
				Capital Allowance	29400

.... ✗

27900

Need to private use balancing allowances & charges

Task 3.5

At the end of the period of account to 31 March 2016, the value of the main pool in Green Ltd's tax computations was £106,000.

On 1 January 2017 a car costing £14,000 was acquired. The CO_2 emissions of the car were 170 g/km, and was used privately 30% of the time by the Finance Director.

There were no other purchases or sales during the year. The company had always prepared accounts to 31 March.

Using the proforma layout provided, calculate the capital allowances available in the year ended 31 March 2017.

	Main	Car	
WDV B/fwd	106000	0	
Addition		14000	
	106000	14000	
WDA 18%	(19080)		
WDA 8%		(1120)	
	86920	12880	
Private use	1120	(336)	784
WDA 18%	19080		
Car	784		
	19864		
			✗

No private use as company

Chapter 4 Computing corporation tax

Task 4.1

Geronimo Ltd's summarised statement of profit or loss for the year ended 31 March 2017 is as follows:

	£	£
Gross profit		925,940
Operating expenses		
Depreciation charge	83,420	
Gifts (note 1)	2,850	
Professional fees (note 2)	14,900	
Repairs and renewals (note 3)	42,310	
Other expenses (all allowable)	165,980	
		(309,460)
Operating profit		616,480
Income from investments		
Debenture interest (note 4)	24,700	
Bank interest (note 4)	4,800	
Dividends (note 5)	56,000	
		85,500
		701,980
Interest payable on loans for trading purposes		(45,000)
Profit for the year before taxation		656,980

Note.

1 Gifts

Gifts are as follows:

	£
Qualifying charitable donation	1,900
Donation to local charity (Geronimo Ltd received free advertising in the charity's magazine)	50
Gifts to customers (food hampers costing £30 each)	900
	2,850

Note.

2 Professional fees

Professional fees are as follows:

	£
Accountancy and audit fee	4,100
Legal fees in connection with the renewal of a 20-year property lease	2,400
Legal fees in connection with the issue of a debenture loan for trade purposes	8,400
	14,900

Note.

3 Repairs and renewals

The figure of £42,310 for repairs includes £6,200 for replacing part of a wall that was knocked down by a lorry, and £12,200 for initial repairs to an office building that was acquired during the year ended 31 March 2017. The office building was not usable until the repairs were carried out, and this fact was represented by a reduced purchase price.

Note.

4 Bank interest

The bank interest and the debenture interest were both received on non-trade investments.

Note.

5 Dividends received

The dividends were received from other companies. The figure of £56,000 is the actual amount received.

Note.

6 Capital allowances

Capital allowances for the year have been calculated as £13,200.

Using the proforma layout provided, calculate Geronimo Ltd's taxable trading profit for the year ended 31 March 2017. Use brackets for deductions and insert 0 (zero) if necessary, in order to fill in all unshaded boxes.

	£	£
Profit per accounts		656,980
	Add	Deduct
Depreciation charge	83420	0
Qualifying charitable donation	0	0
Donation to local charity	0	0
Gifts to customers	900	0
Accountancy and audit fee	0	0
Legal fees – renewal of 20 year lease	0	0
Legal fees – issue of debenture	0	0
Repairs – knocked down wall	0	0
Initial repairs to office	12200	0
Other expenses	0	0
Debenture interest	0	24700
Bank interest	0	4800

	£	£
Dividends	0	56000
Capital allowances	0	13200
Interest payable on trading loans	0	0
Net adjustments		77258
Taxable trading profit		734238

Task 4.2

Decide how each of the following items would be treated in the tax computation of a company with respect to its trading profits. Tick ONE box per line.

	Allow ✓	Disallow and add back ✓	Not taxable as trading income so deduct ✓
Dividends received from an unconnected company			✓
Profit on sale of shares			✓
Running costs of car with 20% private use by an employee	✓		
Parking fine of director		✓	
Capital allowances	✓		
Director's salary	✓		
Bank interest received			✓

Task 4.3

Righteous plc used to make its accounts up to 31 December. However, the directors decided to change the accounting date to 31 May and make up accounts for a 17-month period to 31 May 2017. The following information relates to the period of account from 1 January 2016 to 31 May 2017:

	£
Trading profit	500,000
Property business income	15,300
Capital gain on property sold on:	
1 May 2017	3,000
Qualifying charitable donations paid on:	
28 February 2016	15,000
31 August 2016	15,000
28 February 2017	40,000

No capital allowances are claimed.

Using the proforma layout provided, compute taxable total profits for the accounting periods based on the above accounts. Use brackets for deductions and insert 0 (zero) if necessary, in order to fill in all unshaded boxes.

	Year to 31 December 2016 £	Five months to 31 May 2017 £
Trading profits	352941	147059
Property business income	10800	4500
Chargeable gain	0	3000
Total profits	363741	154559
Qualifying charitable donations paid	(30000)	(40000)
Taxable total profits	333741	114359

Task 4.4

When a company has a period of account which exceeds 12 months, how are the following apportioned:

	Time apportioned ✓	Period in which arises ✓	Separate computation ✓
Capital allowances			✓
Trading income	✓		
Property income	✓		
Interest income	✓		
Chargeable gain		✓	

Interest is in period

Task 4.5

Rosemary Ltd has the following results for the ten-month period ended 31 March 2017:

	£
Taxable trading profits	600,000
Property business income	300,000
Dividends received	162,000

The corporation tax payable by Rosemary Ltd for period ended 31 March 2017 is:

£	180 000

Task 4.6

Cranmore Ltd is a trading company manufacturing specialist engineering tools. It makes up its accounts to 31 December each year.

For the year to 31 December 2016, the company had the following results:

	£
Revenue	525,000
Trading profit before capital allowances	405,000
Interest received from building society deposit	3,000
Property business income from letting out part of factory	16,000
	424,000

The capital allowances have been computed to be £11,000, of which £3,000 is Annual Investment Allowance, £5,500 is writing down allowance on the main pool and £2,500 is writing down allowance on the special rate pool.

Using the above information, show the entries that need to be made on the Form CT600.

Tax calculation

Turnover

Box	Description	Amount
145	**Total turnover from trade**	£ 525000 · 00
150	**Banks, building societies, insurance companies and other financial concerns –** *put an 'X' in this box if you do not have a recognised turnover and have not made an entry in box 145*	☐

Income

Box	Description	Amount
155	**Trading profits**	£ 383000 · 00
160	**Trading losses brought forward claimed against profits**	£ · 00
165	**Net trading profits** – *box 155 minus box 160*	£ 383000 · 00
170	**Bank, building society or other interest, and profits from non-trading loan relationships**	£ 8000 · 00
172	**Put an 'X' in box 172 if the figure in box 170 is net of carrying back a deficit from a later accounting period**	☐
175	**Annual payments not otherwise charged to Corporation Tax and from which Income Tax has not been deducted**	£ · 00
180	**Non-exempt dividends or distributions from non-UK resident companies**	£ · 00
185	**Income from which Income Tax has been deducted**	£ · 00
190	**Income from a property business**	£ 16000 · 00
195	**Non-trading gains on intangible fixed assets**	£ · 00
200	**Tonnage Tax profits**	£ · 00
205	**Income not falling under any other heading**	£ · 00

Chargeable gains

Box	Description	Amount
210	**Gross chargeable gains**	£ · 00
215	**Allowable losses including losses brought forward**	£ · 00
220	**Net chargeable gains** – *box 210 minus box 215*	£ · 00

Profits before deductions and reliefs

Box	Description	Amount
225	**Losses brought forward against certain investment income**	£ · 00
230	**Non-trade deficits on loan relationships (including interest) and derivative contracts (financial instruments) brought forward**	£ · 00
235	**Profits before other deductions and reliefs** – *net sum of boxes 165 to 205 and 220 minus sum of boxes 225 and 230*	£ 402000 · 00

(Adapted from HMRC, 2015)

Chapter 5 Taxing unincorporated businesses

Task 5.1

Rachel commenced in business as a fashion designer on 1 January 2015, and made up her first accounts to 30 April 2016. Her profit for the period, adjusted for taxation, was £33,000. 16 months

Her first tax year is:

1415 ✓

Her taxable profits in her first tax year of trading are:

£ 6187.50 3 months ✓

Her taxable profits in her second tax year of trading are:

£ 24750 ✓

Her taxable profits in her third tax year of trading are:

£ 24750 ✓

Overlap profits are:

£ 22687.50 ✓

Task 5.2

Mr Phone commenced trading on 1 July 2014 making up accounts to 31 May each year.

Profits are:

	£
1 July 2014 to 31 May 2015	22,000
Year ended 31 May 2016	18,000
Year ended 31 May 2017	30,000

Mr Phone's basis period for 2014/15 runs from: (insert the date as xx/xx/xxxx)

1/7/14 ✓

to:

5/4/15

Mr Phone's basis period for 2015/16 runs from: (insert the date as xx/xx/xxxx)

1/7/14

to:

30/6/15

His taxable profits in his second tax year of trading are:

£	23500

Overlap profits are:

18000+1500 = 19500

£	~~18000~~

19500

Task 5.3

Mr Mug ceased trading on 31 December 2016. His overlap profits brought forward amount to £9,000. His profits for the last few periods of account were:

	£
Year ended 30 April 2014 14 15	36,000
Year ended 30 April 2015 15 16	48,000
Year ended 30 April 2016 16 17	16,000
Eight months ended 31 December 2016	4,000

Mr Mug's final tax year is: (insert as xxxx/xx)

16/17

Mr Mug's penultimate tax year is: (insert as xxxx/xx)

15/16

His taxable profits in his final tax year of trading are:

£	11000

16000+4000-9000

Task 5.4

Jackie Smith started her picture framing business on 1 May 2012. Due to falling profits she ceased to trade on 28 February 2017.

Her profits for the whole period of trading were as follows.

	£
1 May 2012 – 31 July 2013	18,000
1 August 2013 – 31 July 2014	11,700
1 August 2014 – 31 July 2015	8,640
1 August 2015 – 31 July 2016	4,800
1 August 2016 – 28 February 2017	5,100

Jackie's first tax year is: (insert as xxxx/xx)

1213

Her taxable profits in her first tax year of trading are:

£ 13200

Jackie's second tax year is: (insert as xxxx/xx)

1314

Her taxable profits in her second tax year of trading are:

£ 14400 1/8/12-31/7/13

Jackie's final tax year is: (insert as xxxx/xx)

1617

Her taxable profits in her final tax year of trading are:

£ 300 4800 + 5100 - 9600

Over the life of her business Jackie is assessed on total profits of:

£ 48240

Task 5.5

Matilda changed her accounting date from 31 March to 31 December. Her accounting periods were as follows:

- Year ended 31 March 2015 1415
- Period ending 31 December 2015 1516
- Year ended 31 December 2016 1617

The year of change for Matilda's business is:

1516

Her basis period for the tax year 14/15 is:

1/4/14 -> 31/3/15

Her basis period for the tax year 15/16 is:

1/1/15 -> 31/12/15

Her basis period for the tax year 16/17 is:

1/1/16 -> 31/12/16

Chapter 6 Partnerships

Task 6.1

Fimbo and Florrie commenced in partnership on 1 January 2015. They produce accounts to 31 December each year and their profits have been as follows:

	Taxable profit £
Year ended 31 December 2015	10,000
Year ended 31 December 2016	20,000
Year ended 31 December 2017	25,000

Until 31 December 2016 Fimbo took 60% of the profits after receiving a £5,000 salary. Florrie took the remaining 40% of profits.

On 1 January 2017, Fimbo and Florrie invite Pom to join the partnership. It is agreed that Fimbo's salary will increase to £6,500 and the profits will then be split equally between the three partners.

Using the proforma layout provided, show the division of profit for the three periods of account. Fill in all unshaded boxes. Insert a 0 (zero) if necessary.

	Total £	Fimbo £	Florrie £	Pom £
12 months to 31 December 2015				
Salary	5000	5000	0	0
Share of profits	5000	3000	2000	0
Total for year	10000	8000	2000	0
12 months to 31 December 2016				
Salary	5000	5000	0	0
Share of profits	15000	9000	6000	0
Total for year	20000	14000	6000	0
12 months to 31 December 2017				
Salary	6500	6500	0	0
Share of profits	18500	6167	6167	6167
Total for year	25000	12667	6167	6167

Task 6.2

John, Paul and George began to trade as partners on 1 January 2014. The profits of the partnership are shared in the ratio 4:3:3. The accounts for recent periods have shown the following results:

	£
Period to 31 July 2014	24,300
Year to 31 July 2015	16,200
Year to 31 July 2016	14,900

(a) Using the proforma layout provided, show the allocation of trading profits for all three periods of account. Fill in all unshaded boxes. Insert a 0 (zero) if necessary.

	Total £	John £	Paul £	George £
Period ended 31 July 2014				
Division of profits	24300	9720	7290	7290
Year ended 31 July 2015				
Division of profits	16200	6480	4860	4860
Year ended 31 July 2016				
Division of profits	14900	5960	4470	4470

(b) Using the proforma layout provided, calculate the taxable trading profits of John, Paul and George for all tax years. Fill in all boxes.

	John £	Paul £	George £
2013/14 1/1/14 - 5/4/14	4166	3124	3124
2014/15 1/1/14 - 31/12/15	12420	9315	9315
2015/16	6480	4860	4860
2016/17	5960	4470	4470

Task 6.3

Strange and his partners Pavin and Lehman had traded for many years. Strange had contributed £20,000 to the business and Pavin £10,000.

Profits were shared in the ratio of 3:2:1 after providing Strange and Pavin with salaries of £15,000 and £5,000 and interest on capital of 5%.

On 1 August 2016 the profit sharing arrangements were changed to 2:2:1 after providing only Strange with a salary of £20,000, and no further interest on capital for any of the partners.

The partnership profit for the year to 31 December 2016 was £48,000.

Using the proforma layout provided, show the allocation of profit for the year to 31 December 2016. Fill in all unshaded boxes. Insert a 0 (zero) if necessary.

Year ended 31 December 2016	Total £	Strange £	Pavin £	Lehman £
To 31 July 2016				
Salaries	11667	8750	2917	0
Interest on capital	875	583	292	0
Division of profits	15458	7729	5153	2576
To 31 December 2016				
Salary	8333	8333	0	0
Division of profits	11667	4667	4667	2333
Total for year ended 31 December 2016	48000	30062	13029	4909

7 months

5 months

Task 6.4

Bob, Annie and John started their partnership on 1 June 2010 and make accounts up to 31 May each year. The accounts have always shown taxable profits.

For the period up to 31 January 2016 each partner received a salary of £15,000 per annum and the remaining profits were shared 50% to Bob and 25% each to Annie and John. There was no interest on capital.

Bob left the partnership on 1 February 2016. The profit sharing ratio, after the same salaries, changed to 50% each to Annie and John.

Profits for the year ending 31 May 2016 were £90,000.

Using the proforma layout provided, calculate each partner's share of the profits for the year to 31 May 2016. Fill in all unshaded boxes. Insert a 0 (zero) if necessary.

Year ended 31 May 2016	Total £	Bob £	Annie £	John £
8/12 **To 31 January 2016**				
Salaries	30000	10000	10000	10000
Division of profits	30000	15000	7500	7500
4/12 **To 31 May 2016**				
Salaries	10000	0	5000	5000
Division of profits	20000	0	10000	10000
Total for year ended 31 May 2016	90000	25000	32500	32500

✓

Task 6.5

This style of task is human marked in the live assessment.

Anne Curtis and Bettina Stone have been trading in partnership selling designer dresses for many years, making up accounts to 31 December each year. They share profits equally.

The following information relates to the year to 31 December 2016:

	£
Revenue	125,000
Cost of goods bought	75,000
Rental of shop	12,000
General administration	1,700
Accountancy	650
Goods taken for own use (market value)	1,550
New sewing machine for alterations	1,200
The partnership received interest in the year to 5 April 2017 of:	
Gross bank interest received (including tax credit)	8,000
Tax deducted on bank interest	1,600

Using this information, complete page 6 of the Partnership Tax return which follows for Anne Curtis.

PARTNERSHIP STATEMENT (SHORT) *for the year ended 5 April 2017*

Please read these instructions before completing the Statement

Use these pages to allocate partnership income if the only income for the relevant return period was trading and professional income or taxed interest and alternative finance receipts from banks and building societies. Otherwise you must download or ask the SA Orderline for the *Partnership Statement (Full)* pages to record details of the allocation of all the partnership income. Go to **hmrc.gov.uk/selfassessmentforms**

Step 1 Fill in boxes 1 to 29 and boxes A and B as appropriate. Get the figures you need from the relevant boxes in the Partnership Tax Return. Complete a separate Statement for each accounting period covered by this Partnership Tax Return and for each trade or profession carried on by the partnership.

Step 2 Then allocate the amounts in boxes 11 to 29 attributable to each partner using the allocation columns on this page and page 7, read the Partnership Tax Return Guide, go to **hmrc.gov.uk/selfassessmentforms** If the partnership has more than three partners, please photocopy page 7.

Step 3 Each partner will need a copy of their allocation of income to fill in their personal tax return.

PARTNERSHIP INFORMATION

If the partnership business includes a trade or profession, enter here the accounting period for which appropriate items in this statement are returned.

Start **1** 1 / 1 / 16

End **2** 31 / 12 / 16

Nature of trade **3** Selling designer dresses

MIXED PARTNERSHIPS

Tick here if this Statement is drawn up using Corporation Tax rules **4** ☐

Tick here if this Statement is drawn up using tax rules for non-residents **5** ☐

Individual partner details

6 Name of partner Anne Curtis

Address

Postcode

Date appointed as a partner (if during 2014–15 or 2015–16) **7** / /

Partner's Unique Taxpayer Reference (UTR) **8**

Date ceased to be a partner (if during 2014–15 or 2015–16) **9** / /

Partner's National Insurance number **10**

Partnership's profits, losses, income, tax credits, etc.	Tick this box if the items entered in the box had foreign tax taken off		*Partner's share of profits, losses, income, tax credits, etc.*	*Copy figures in boxes 11 to 29 to boxes in the individual's* ***Partnership (short)*** *pages as shown below*
• for an accounting period ended in 2016/17				
from box 3.83 Profit from a trade or profession	**A** ☐	**11** £ 36000	Profit **11** £ 18000	*Copy this figure to box 8*
from box 3.82 Adjustment on change of basis		**11A** £	**11A** £	*Copy this figure to box 10*
from box 3.84 Loss from a trade or profession	**B** ☐	**12** £	Loss **12** £	*Copy this figure to box 8*
from box 10.4 Business Premises Renovation Allowance		**12A** £	**12A** £	*Copy this figure to box 15*
• for the period 6 April 2015 to 5 April 2016/17				
from box 7.9A UK taxed interest and taxed alternative finance receipts		**22** £ 8000	**22** £ 4000	*Copy this figure to box 28*
from box 3.97 CIS deductions made by contractors on account of tax		**24** £	**24** £	*Copy this figure to box 30*
from box 3.98 Other tax taken off trading income		**24A** £	**24A** £	*Copy this figure to box 31*
from box 7.8A Income Tax taken off		**25** £	**25** £	*Copy this figure to box 29*
from box 3.117 Partnership charges		**29** £	**29** £	*Copy this figure to box 4, 'Other tax reliefs' section on page Ai 2 in your personal tax return*

** if you are a 'CT Partnership' see the Partnership Tax Return Guide*

SA800 2016 PARTNERSHIP TAX RETURN: PAGE 6

(Adapted from HMRC, 2016)

Chapter 7 National insurance

Task 7.1

Abraham has trading profits of £12,830 for the year ended 31 December 2016.

The Class 2 NIC liability for 2016/17 is:

£	145	.	60

✓

The Class 4 NIC liability for 2016/17 is:

£	429	.	30

✓

The total NIC liability for 2016/17 is:

£	574	.	90

✓

Task 7.2

John has profits of £48,000 for the year ended 31 March 2017.

The Class 2 NIC liability for 2016/17 is:

£	145	.	60

✓

The Class 4 NIC liability for 2016/17 is:

£	3244	.	60

✓

The total NIC liability for 2016/17 is:

£	3390	.	20

✓

Task 7.3

Raj has trading profits of £3,500 for 2016/17.

The Class 2 NIC liability for 2016/17 is:

£	0	.	00

✓

The Class 4 NIC liability for 2016/17 is:

£	0	.	00

✓

The total NIC liability for 2016/17 is:

£	0	.	00

✓

Task 7.4

Zoë is a self employed author who starts in business on 6 April 2016. In the year to 5 April 2017 she had taxable trading profits of £80,000.

The Class 2 NIC liability for 2016/17 is:

£	145	.	60

✓

The Class 4 NIC liability for 2016/17 is:

£	3664	.	60

✗

The total NIC liability for 2016/17 is:

£	3810	.	20

✗

Do not include personal allowance

Task 7.5

Wendy and Jayne have been in partnership as interior designers for many years, trading as Dramatic Decors.

On 1 January 2017, Wendy and Jayne admitted Paula to the partnership. From that date, partnership profits were shared 40% to each of Wendy and Jayne and 20% to Paula. The partnership continued to make up its accounts to 31 December and the trading profit for the year to 31 December 2017 was £180,000.

Paula had not worked for many years prior to becoming a partner in Dramatic Decors.

(a) The share of profits taxable on Paula for 2016/17 is:

£	9000

✓

and for 2017/18 is:

£	36000

✓

and the overlap profits to carry forward are:

£	9000

✓

(b) The Class 4 NIC payable by Paula for 2016/17 are:

£	84	.	60

Chapter 8 Losses

Task 8.1

Pipchin has traded for many years, making up accounts to 30 September each year. His recent results have been:

Year ended	£
30 September 2014	12,000
30 September 2015	(45,000)
30 September 2016	8,000
30 September 2017	14,000

He has received property income as follows:

	£
2014/15	10,400
2015/16	11,000
2016/17	11,000
2017/18	11,000

Using the proforma layout provided, compute Pipchin's net income for 2014/15 to 2017/18, assuming maximum claims for loss relief are made as early as possible. If an answer is zero, insert 0, and show the offset of losses within brackets. Fill in all boxes.

	2014/15 £	2015/16 £	2016/17 £	2017/18 £
Trading profits	12000	0	8000	14000
Trading loss offset against future year	0	0	(8000)	(3600)
Property income	10400	11000	11000	11000
Trading loss offset against current year	0	(11060)	0	0
Trading loss offset against previous year	(22400)	0	0	0
Net income	0	0	11000	21400

Task 8.2

Identify whether the following statement is true or false.

An individual can restrict a claim to set a trading loss against total income in order to have enough net income to use his personal allowance.

	✓
True	
False	✓

Task 8.3

Identify whether the following statement is true or false.

An individual must make a trading loss claim against total income in the tax year of the loss before making a claim to set the loss against total income in the preceding year.

	✓
True	
False	✓

Task 8.4

Identify whether the following statement is true or false.

An individual can only carry a trading loss forward against trading income of the same trade.

	✓
True	✓
False	

Task 8.5

Pennington Ltd produced the following results:

	Year ended 30 June		
	2014 £	2015 £	2016 £
Trading profit/(loss)	62,000	20,000	(83,000)
Interest income	1,200	600	1,200
Qualifying charitable donation	100	50	100

(a) Using the proforma layout provided, compute Pennington Ltd's taxable total profits for the above accounting periods, assuming the loss relief is claimed as soon as possible. Fill in all boxes. Use brackets for loss relief and add a 0 (zero) where necessary.

	Year ended 30 June		
	2014	2015	2016
Trading profits	62000	20000	0
Interest	1200	600	1200
Total profits	63200	20600	1200
Current period loss relief	0	0	(1200)
Carry back loss relief	0	(20600)	0
Total profits after loss relief	63200	0	0
Qualifying charitable donation	(100)	(50)	(100)
Taxable total profits	63100	0	0

✓

(b) The trading loss available to carry forward at 30 June 2016 is:

£	61200

✓

Task 8.6

Ferraro Ltd has the following results.

	Year ended 30.9.14 £	9 months to 30.6.15 £	Year ended 30.6.16 £	Year ended 30.6.17 £
Trading profit (loss)	6,200	4,320	(100,000)	53,000
Bank deposit interest accrued	80	240	260	200
Rents receivable	1,420	1,440	1,600	1,500
Chargeable gain	–	12,680	–	–
Allowable capital loss	(5,000)	–	(9,423)	
Qualifying charitable donation	1,000	1,000	1,500	1,500

(a) Using the proforma layout provided, compute all taxable total profits, claiming loss reliefs as early as possible. Fill in all boxes. Use brackets for loss relief and add a 0 (zero) where necessary.

	Year ended 30.9.14	9 months to 30.6.15	Year ended 30.6.16	Year ended 30.6.17
Trading profits	6200	4320	0	53000
Carry forward loss relief	0	0	0	(53000)
Interest	80	240	260	200
Property income	1420	1440	1600	1500
Chargeable gains	0	7680	0	0
Total profits	7700	13680	1860	1700
Current period loss relief	0	[illegible]	(1860)	0

	Year ended 30.9.14	9 months to 30.6.15	Year ended 30.6.16	Year ended 30.6.17
Carry back loss relief	(1925)	(13680)	0	0
Total profits after loss relief	5775	0	0	1700
Qualifying charitable donation	(1000)	(1000)	(1500)	(1500)
Taxable total profits	4775	0	0	200

(b) The trading loss available to carry forward at 30 June 2017 is:

£	29535

(c) The capital loss available to carry forward at 30 June 2017 is:

£	9423

Task 8.7

Identify whether the following statement is true or false.

A company must offset its trading loss against total profits in the loss-making period before carrying the loss back.

	✓
True	✓
False	

Task 8.8

Identify whether the following statement is true or false.

If a company carries a trading loss forward, the loss can be set against total profits in the following accounting period.

	✓
True	
False	✓

Task 8.9

Identify whether the following statement is true or false.

A company can set-off a capital loss against trading profits.

	✓
True	
False	✓

Chapter 9 Self assessment for individuals

Task 9.1

Identify by which date an individual should normally submit his 2016/17 self-assessment tax return if it is to be filed online. Tick ONE box.

	✓
31 January 2018	✓
5 April 2018	
31 October 2017	
31 December 2017	

Task 9.2

Gordon had income tax payable of £14,500 in 2015/16. His income tax payable for 2016/17 was £20,500.

How will Gordon settle his income tax payable for 2016/17? Tick ONE box.

	✓
The full amount of £20,500 will be paid on 31 January 2018.	
Payments on account based on the estimated 2016/17 liability will be made on 31 January and 31 July 2017, with the balance payable on 31 January 2018.	
Payments on account of £10,250 will be made on 31 January and 31 July 2017 with nothing due on 31 January 2018.	
Payments on account of £7,250 will be made on 31 January and 31 July 2017, with the balance of £6,000 being paid on 31 January 2018.	✓

Task 9.3

The minimum penalty as a percentage of Potential Lost Revenue for a deliberate and concealed error on a tax return where there is a prompted disclosure is:

	✓
100%	
50%	✓
35%	
15%	

Task 9.4

The maximum penalty as a percentage of Potential Lost Revenue for careless error for failure to notify chargeability is:

	✓
0%	
20%	
30%	✓
35%	

Task 9.5

Identify whether the following statement is true or false.

If an individual files her 2016/17 return online on 13 April 2018, the penalty for late filing is £100.

	✓
True	✓
False	

Task 9.6

Identify whether the following statement is true or false.

The penalty for failure to keep records is £3,000 per tax year or accounting period.

	✓
True	✓
False	

Task 9.7

Identify whether the following statement is true or false.

An individual is required to make a payment on account on 31 July 2017 for 2016/17. The payment is actually made on 10 November 2017.

The penalty payable is 5%.

	✓
True	
False	✓

Chapter 10 Self assessment for companies

Task 10.1

Boscobel plc has been a large company for corporation tax purposes for many years. For the year ending 31 March 2017, it had a corporation tax liability of £500,000.

Fill in the table below showing how it will pay its corporation tax liability.

Instalment	Due date (xx/xx/xxxx)	Amount due £
1	14/10/16	125 000
2	14/1/17	125 000
3	14/4/17	125000
4	14/7/17	125000

Task 10.2

Tick whether the following statements are true or false.

	True ✓	False ✓
A company with a period of account ending on 31 March 2017 must keep its records until 31 March 2019.		✓
The due date for payment of CGT for 2016/17 is 31 January 2018.	✓	
An individual who becomes chargeable to income tax in 2016/17 must notify HMRC by 31 October 2017.		✓
A large company will not have to pay corporation tax by instalments if it has profits not exceeding £10m and was not large in the previous accounting period.	✓	
A company which is not large (for corporation tax purposes) must pay its corporation tax by nine months and one day after the end of its accounting period.	✓	

Task 10.3

A company receives a notice to file its return for the year ended 31 December 2016 on 28 November 2017.

The corporation tax return must be filed by:

28/2/18

31/12/17 or 28/2/18

A company receives a notice to file its return for the year ended 30 June 2016 on 15 July 2016.

The corporation tax return must be filed by:

~~15/7/16~~

30/6/17

Task 10.4

A company must keep its accounting records for 6 **years.**

Failure to do so may incur a penalty of £ 3000.

Task 10.5

Fred works as an IT Consultant and derives nearly all of his income from one main client, Bishopston Ltd. Fred uses his Personal Service Company, Fred Services Ltd to invoice Bishopston Ltd, and then extracts most of the income from his company via dividends. Fred works from home, using a Bishopston Ltd laptop and is permitted under the agreement with Bishopston Ltd to get someone else to perform the work when he is on holiday or unwell.

Explain which aspects of this scenario suggest that the IR35 rules may or may not apply.

May
One main client
Extracts most income via dividends
Company laptop
Holiday & sickness terms.

This suggest not

Explain what difference it would make to how Fred is taxed if the IR35 rules are imposed.

An additional employment income tax charge would be placed on Fred ✓

Subject to tax & NIC

Task 10.6

A small company spends £50,000 on Research and Development staff and consumables in the year ended 30 June 2016.

The amount which is deductible as a trading expense is

£	115000

. ✓

If this resulted in a loss, the loss could be surrendered in exchange for a tax credit at the rate of 5·3 **%** 14·5%

Chapter 11 Chargeable gains – the basics

Task 11.1

Complete the following sentence by filling in the gaps:

For the gain on the disposal of a capital asset to be a chargeable gain there must be a chargeable disposal **of a chargeable** asset **by a chargeable** person.

Task 11.2

Identify whether the following assets are chargeable assets or exempt assets for CGT:

Item	Chargeable ✓	Exempt ✓
Wasting chattel with useful life of 25 years		✓
Disposal of half the holding of a plot of land	✓	
Car used for business purposes	✓	

Task 11.3

Romana purchased a freehold holiday cottage for £40,000. She then spent £5,000 on a new conservatory. She sold the cottage for £90,000 on 15 March 2017. Romana had not made any other disposals during 2016/17.

What is her taxable gain for 2016/17?

	✓
£33,900	
£38,900	
£45,000	✓
£50,000	

Annual exempt amount

Task 11.4

In August 2016 George made chargeable gains of £20,000 and allowable losses of £3,560. He made no other disposals during 2016/17 and he is a higher rate taxpayer.

(a) George's capital gains tax liability for 2016/17 is:

£	1068

✓

(b) George's capital gains tax liability is payable by:

31/1/18

✓

Task 11.5

Jack sells a residential property in December 2016 and makes a chargeable gain of £15,000. Jack is a higher rate taxpayer.

At what rate would Jack pay capital gains tax on this gain?

£	28%

✓

Task 11.6

In November 2016, Graham made chargeable gains of £15,000 and allowable losses of £5,200. He made no other disposals during 2016/17.

The amount of the loss Graham will use in 2016/17 is:

£	3900

✗ cannot restrict current year loss

Task 11.7

Gayle made chargeable gains of £5,000 in August 2016 and £17,500 in November 2016. In July 2016 she made allowable losses of £2,000. She has unused basic rate band of £5,000 in 2016/17.

Gayle's capital gains tax liability for 2016/17 is:

£	1380

✓

9400

5000 × 10% = 500

4400 × 20% = 880

Task 11.8

Gerry made chargeable gains of £27,100 in December 2016. She made no other disposals in the year. Her taxable income (ie after deducting the personal allowance) for 2016/17 was £23,005. Note the limit for the basic rate band for 2016/17 is £32,000.

Gerry's capital gains tax liability for 2016/17 is:

£	2300.50

Task 11.9

Kevin made gains of £18,900 and losses of £6,600 in 2016/17. He has losses brought forward of £5,000.

The losses to carry forward to 2017/18 are:

£	3800

Task 11.10

Elias has the following gains and losses arising from disposals of chargeable assets:

Tax year	2014/15 £	2015/16 £	2016/17 £
Gains	2,000	4,000	13,700
Losses	(14,000)	(2,000)	(2,000)

The maximum allowable loss carried forward to 2017/18 will be:

£	15400

Task 11.11

On 14 April 2016, Fire Ltd sold a factory for £230,000. This had originally been purchased in April 2001 for £160,000.

Assumed Indexation factor

April 2001 – April 2016 0.514

Using the proforma layout provided calculate the chargeable gain arising on the disposal of the factory. Fill in all boxes. Add a 0 (zero) if necessary.

	£
Proceeds	230000
Less cost	(160 000)
Unindexed gain	70000
Less indexation allowance	(70000)
Chargeable gain/allowable loss	0

Task 11.12

On 18 July 2016, Earth plc sold a warehouse for £180,000. This had been purchased in May 2006 for £100,000. Earth plc had spent £25,000 on an extension to the warehouse in August 2008.

Assumed Indexation factors

May 2006 – July 2016	0.345
May 2006 – August 2008	0.080
August 2008 – July 2016	0.246

Using the proforma layout provided calculate the chargeable gain arising on the disposal of the warehouse. Fill in all boxes. Add a 0 (zero) if necessary.

	£
Proceeds	180000
Less: cost	(100000)
enhancement expenditure	(25000)
Unindexed gain	55000
Less: indexation allowance on cost	(34500)
indexation allowance on enhancement	(6150)
Chargeable gain	14350

Task 11.13

Identify whether the following statement is true or false.

A company is entitled to an annual exempt amount.

	✓
True	
False	✓

Chapter 12 Further aspects of chargeable gains

Task 12.1

Harry bought a three-acre plot of land for £150,000. He sold two acres of the land at auction for £240,000. His disposal costs were £3,000. The market value of the one remaining acre at the date of sale was £60,000.

(a) The cost of the land sold is:

£	120000

✓

(b) The gain on sale is:

£	87000

✗ 117000

Task 12.2

Leonora purchased a picture for £5,500 and sold it in September for £7,500, incurring £300 expenses of sale.

Her chargeable gain on sale is:

	✓
£2,300	
£2,000	
£2,500	
£1,700	✓

1700 or 2500

✓

Task 12.3

Mark purchased an antique vase for £9,000. He sold the vase in August at auction for £4,500 net of auctioneer's fees of 10%.

Mark's allowable loss is:

5000

£	3000

3500

Task 12.4

Identify whether the following statement is true or false.

Chloe bought a necklace for £4,000. She sold it in September for £5,500.

Chloe has a chargeable gain on sale of £1,500.

	✓
True	
False	✓

✓

Task 12.5

In August 2016, John gave his daughter an asset worth £10,000. He had acquired the asset for £25,000.

In March 2017, John gave his brother an asset worth £60,000. John had acquired the asset for £15,000.

John's chargeable gains (before the annual exempt amount) for 2016/17 are:

	✓
£45,000	
£30,000	✓
£34,100	
£19,100	

45000 ✗

Can only offset loss against same connected person

Task 12.6

Identify whether the following statement is true or false.

A disposal to a connected person is deemed to be at market value.

	✓
True	✓
False	

✓

Task 12.7

On 14 November 2016, Wind plc sold two offices for £140,000. These had been part of a large office block. The whole block had cost £250,000 in August 2003 and in November 2016 the remaining offices had a market value of £320,000.

Assumed indexation factor:

August 2003 – November 2016 0.468

(a) The cost of the two offices disposed of is:

£	~~103488~~ 76087 ✓

(b) The chargeable gain arising on the disposal is:

£	~~40128~~ 28304 ✓

Task 12.8

LM plc bought a painting in October 2008 for £4,500. It sold the painting at auction in September 2016 and received £7,500 after deducting the auctioneers' commission of £500. Assume the indexation factor between October 2008 and September 2016 is 0.238.

Complete the following computation.

	£
Proceeds	8000
Disposal costs	(500)
Cost of acquisition	(4500)
Indexation allowance	(1071)
Gain	1929
Gain using chattel marginal relief	3333
Chargeable gain	1929

✓

Chapter 13 Share disposals

Task 13.1

Jake sold 5,000 ordinary shares for £20,000 in JKL plc on 10 August 2016. He bought 6,000 shares in JKL plc for £9,000 on 15 July 2014 and another 1,000 shares for £4,200 on 16 August 2016.

His net gain on sale is:

£	9800

20000
10200
9800

1000
4000

4200
6000
10200

Task 13.2

Susan's dealings in K plc were as follows:

	No. of shares	Cost/(proceeds) £
10 February 2001	12,000	18,000
20 September 2008	Bonus issue of 1 for 4	Nil
15 March 2017	(2,000)	(8,000)

Using the proforma layout provided, calculate the gain on sale. Fill in all unshaded boxes. Use a 0 (zero) if necessary.

Share pool

	No. of shares	Cost £
10 February 2001	12000	18000
20 September 2008 Bonus 1:4	3000	0
Total before disposal	15000	18000
15 March 2017 Disposal	(2000)	(2400)
c/f	13000	15600

Gain on sale

	£
Proceeds	8000
Less cost	(2400)
Gain	5600

Task 13.3

This style of task is human marked in the live assessment.

Geoff sold 10,000 of his shares in AC plc on 4 November 2016 for £60,000. The shares had been acquired as follows:

	No. of shares	Cost £
9 December 2001	12,000	4,400
12 October 2005 (rights issue 1:3 at £5)		
10 November 2016	2,000	11,500

Compute the gain or loss made on these shares. Clearly show the balance of shares and their value to carry forward.

	No Shares	£
9/12/01	12000	4400
Rights issue	4000	20000
Total before disposal	16000	24400
Disposal	(8000)	(12200)
C fwd	8000	12200
Pk		

Proceeds	60000	
Cost 10/11/16	(11500)	
Sharepool	(12200)	
	36300	✓

Task 13.4

Standring Ltd owned 20,000 shares in Smart plc acquired as follows:

5,000 shares acquired September 2001 for £10,000.
1 for 5 rights acquired October 2004 at £5 per share.
14,000 shares acquired August 2006 for £84,000.
Standring Ltd sold 18,000 shares in January 2017 for £155,000.

Indexation factors

September 2001 – October 2004	0.080
October 2004 – August 2006	0.056
August 2006 – January 2017	0.323

Using the proforma layout provided, calculate the chargeable gain arising on the sale in January 2017.

FA 1985 pool

	Shares	Cost	IC
Addition Sept 01	5000	10000	10000
Index to Oct 04	0	0	800
	5000	10000	10800
Rights issue	1000	5000	5000
	6000	15000	15800
Index to Aug 06	0	0	885
	6000	15000	16685
Addition Aug 06	14000	84000	84000
	20000	99000	100685
Index to Jan 17	0	0	32521
	20000	99000	133206

	Share	Cost	IC
	20000	99000	133206
Disposal	(18000)	(89100)	(119885)
	2000	9900	13321

Gain

Proceeds	155000
Cost	(89100)
Unindexed gain	65900
Indexation	(30785)
Gain	35115

Task 13.5

Box plc sold 11,000 shares in Crate Ltd for £78,200 on 25 May 2016. These shares had been acquired as follows.

26 May 1995	Purchased	4,000 shares for	£24,000
30 June 1996	1 for 2 bonus issue		
24 October 2003	Purchased	5,000 shares for	£27,500

Indexation factors

May 1995 – October 2003	0.221
May 1995 – June 1996	0.023
June 1996 – October 2003	0.193
October 2003 – May 2016	0.428

Using the proforma layout provided, calculate the gain on disposal.

FA 1985 pool

	Shares	Cost	IC
26/5/95	4000	24000	24000
~~Index~~ Bonus	2000	0	0
Total at June 96	6000	24000	24000
Index to Oct 03	0	0	4632
	6000	24000	28632
Addition	5000	27500	27500

Total	11000	51500	56132
Index	0	0	24024
	11000	51500	80156
Disposal	(11000)	(51500)	(80156)
	0	0	0

Gain

Proceeds	78200
Cost	(51500)
Unindexed gain	26700
Indexation	(28656)
Gain	0

Task 13.6

Identify whether the following statement is true or false.

Indexation allowance on rights issue shares runs from the date of the rights issue even though the rights issue shares are treated as having been acquired at the time of the original acquisition to which they relate.

	✓
True	✓
False	

Chapter 14 Reliefs for chargeable gains

Task 14.1

Ronald started in business as a sole trader in August 2007. He acquired a freehold shop for £80,000 and a warehouse for £150,000.

He sold his business as a going concern to Lesley in December 2016 and received £50,000 for goodwill, £90,000 for the shop and £130,000 for the warehouse. Ronald made no other chargeable gains in 2016/17 and he is a higher rate taxpayer.

Using the proforma layout provided, compute the CGT payable by Ronald for 2016/17. Fill in all unshaded boxes. Use a 0 (zero) if necessary.

	£	£
Proceeds of goodwill	50000	
Less cost	–	
Gain/(loss) on goodwill		50000
Proceeds of shop	90000	
Less cost	(80000)	
Gain/(loss) on shop		10000
Proceeds of warehouse	130000	
Less cost	(150000)	
Gain/(loss) on warehouse		(20000)
Net gains eligible for entrepreneurs' relief		40000
Less annual exempt amount		(11100)
Taxable gains		28900
CGT payable		2890

Task 14.2

Identify whether the following statement is true or false.

The lifetime limit of gains eligible for entrepreneurs' relief is £10,000,000.

	✓
True	✓
False	

Task 14.3

Simon acquired 10,000 Blue Ltd shares worth £65,000 in September 1992 as a gift from his father. His father had originally acquired them as an investment in 1987 and gift relief was claimed on the gain of £15,000. Simon sold the Blue Ltd shares for £200,000 on 30 November 2016. He has no other assets for CGT purposes and made no other disposals in 2016/17.

The taxable gain arising on the sale of the Blue Ltd shares is:

£	138900

65000
50000
15000

200000
50000
150000

Task 14.4

Fran gave a factory worth £500,000 to her friend Anna on 1 June 2016 and a claim for gift relief was made. Fran had bought the factory on 1 January 1997 for £75,000. On 1 July 2017 Anna sold the factory for £520,000.

(a) Fran's chargeable gain on her disposal is:

£	nil

500000
75000
425000

(b) Anna's chargeable gain on her disposal is:

£	445000

520000
75000
445000

Task 14.5

On 6 April 1989 Edward acquired for £60,000 a small workshop where he carried on his trade as a furniture maker. On 6 August 2016 he sold the workshop for £125,000 having moved on 10 April 2016 to smaller premises which cost £123,500.

(a) Edward's gain on the disposal before rollover relief is:

£	63000

✓

(b) Assuming rollover relief is claimed, the gain immediately chargeable is:

£	1500

✓

(c) The gain which Edward can rollover into the new premises is:

£	63500

✓

Task 14.6

On 23 May 2013 Del Ltd sold a freehold property for £145,000 which had cost originally £50,000 on 9 May 2001. On 15 April 2016 Del Ltd acquired the freehold of another property for £140,000. Rollover relief was claimed.

Indexation factor

May 2001 – May 2013 0.435

145000
50000
21750
73250

(a) The gain on disposal in May 2013 was:

£	73250

✓

(b) The gain available for rollover relief is:

£	68250

✓

(c) The base cost of the property acquired in April 2016 is:

£	71750

✓

Task 14.7

L plc sold a plot of land.

Tick the box that correctly finishes the following statement.

If L plc wishes to claim rollover relief it must acquire a new asset between:

	✓
The start of the previous accounting period and the end of the next accounting period	
Three years before and three years after the date of the disposal	
One year before and three years after the date of the disposal	✓
One year before and one year after the date of the disposal	

Answer Bank

Chapter 1 Tax framework

Task 1.1

	Incorporated ✓	Unincorporated ✓
Sole trader		✓
Partnership		✓
Limited company	✓	

Task 1.2

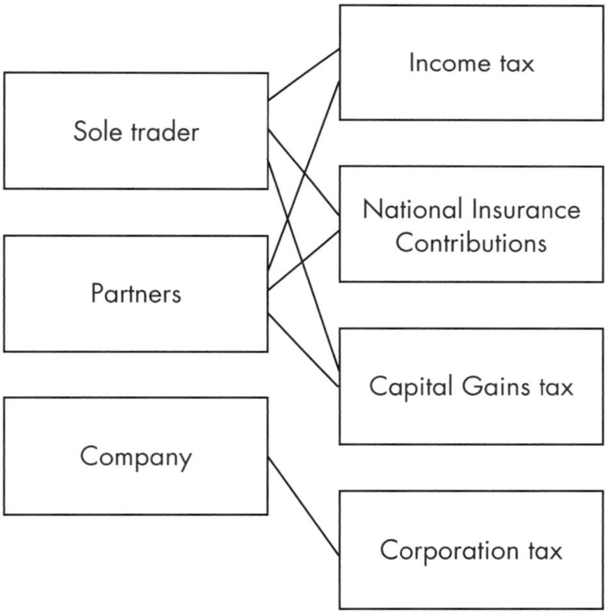

Task 1.3

	Force of law ✓	No force of law ✓
Statute law	✓	
Act of Parliament	✓	
Statutory Instrument	✓	
HMRC guidance		✓
Case Law	✓	

Task 1.4

	✓
Claiming capital allowances on a fictitious piece of equipment	
Failing to notify HMRC of a profitable trade commenced three years ago	
Obtaining tax-free interest by investing in an ISA	✓
Deciding not to declare rental income received	

Task 1.5

Ethical duties and responsibilities of an AAT accountant (Any two of the following):

Maintain client confidentiality at all times
Adopt an ethical approach and maintain an objective outlook
Give timely and constructive advice to clients
Honest and professional conduct with HMRC

Task 1.6

Tax [avoidance] is the use of loopholes in tax legislation to minimise tax liabilities.

Tax [planning] is the use of all available reliefs in the manner intended to minimise tax liabilities.

Tax [evasion] is the deliberate misleading of tax authorities to minimise tax liabilities.

Chapter 2 Computing trading income

Task 2.1

From:	AAT student
To:	A Client
Date:	14 June
Subject:	Badges of trade

In order to decide whether a trade is being carried on the following 'badges of trade' need to be considered:

(a) **Subject matter.** When people engage in trade, they frequently do so by purchasing and re-selling objects with a view to making a profit. Objects bought for this purpose are often not the type of objects that would be bought for investment or enjoyment. This means that the subject matter of a transaction will very often indicate whether a trade is being carried on or not.

(b) **Length of ownership.** A short period of ownership is an indication of an intention to trade in a commodity.

(c) **Frequency of transactions.** Where the same type of article is repeatedly bought and sold, it will normally suggest that there is trading in that article.

(d) **Supplementary work** on or in connection with the property sold, eg modification, processing, packaging, or renovating the item sold suggests the carrying on of a trade.

(e) **Acquisition of asset.** If goods are acquired deliberately, trading may be indicated. If goods are acquired by gift or inheritance, their later sale is unlikely to constitute trading.

(f) **Profit motive.** This is usually the most important consideration though its absence does not prevent a trade being carried on if, in fact, the operation is run on commercial lines and a profit does result.

These **badges of trade** are only general indications and, in each case, all the facts must be considered before any decision can be made.

Task 2.2

	Allow ✓	Disallow and add back ✓	Not taxable so deduct ✓
Gifts of 30 bottles of wine to clients		✓	
Lease costs of a car with emissions of 150g/km		✓ (15%)	
Costs of £5,000 to repair a roof	✓		
£1,000 cost to register a patent	✓		
Accounting profit on disposal of a van			✓
£500 donation to a political party		✓	
Repair to factory roof	✓		

Task 2.3

	£	£
Profit for the year per accounts		5,300
	Add	Deduct
Staff wages	0	0
Mr Jelly's salary (N1)	260	0
Light and heat	0	0
Motor expenses (N2) (£350 × 1/7)	50	0
Postage, stationery and telephone	0	0
Painting shop internally	0	0
Plant repairs	0	0
Stockroom extension (N3)	101	0
Provision (N4)	200	0
Donations (N2)	10	0
Advertising	0	0
Entertaining (N5)	90	0
Gifts (N6)	70	0
Legal expenses	0	0
Depreciation charge	600	0
Total net adjustments		1,381
Taxable trading profit		6,681

Notes

1 Appropriation of profit
2 Not expenditure incurred wholly and exclusively for the purpose of trade
3 Capital items
4 Increase in general provision is disallowed
5 Entertaining expenses specifically disallowed
6 Gifts of alcohol specifically disallowed

Task 2.4

	Allow ✓	Disallow and add back ✓	Not taxable so deduct ✓
Increase in specific provision	✓		
Decrease in general provision			✓
Depreciation charge		✓	
Cocktail party held for customers		✓	
Political donation		✓	
Employees salary	✓		
Repair to factory roof	✓		

Task 2.5

Box 17	£25,000
Box 21	£1,760
Box 23	£1,700
Box 26	£150
Box 28	£1,650
Box 31	£30,260
Box 43	£500
Box 46	£500

Chapter 3 Capital allowances

Task 3.1

	Revenue ✓	Capital ✓
Purchase of machinery		✓
Rent paid for premises	✓	
Insurance of premises	✓	
Repairs to roof of factory	✓	
New extension to shop		✓
Purchase of new car for owner		✓
Legal fees relating to purchase of new factory		✓
Payment of staff wages	✓	
Accountancy costs	✓	
Redecoration of shop	✓	

Task 3.2

	AIA £	Main pool £	Mercedes car (80%) £	Allowance £
Y/e 30 June 2016				
b/f		38,500		
Additions				
14.1.16 Furniture	23,800			
30.3.16 Car			18,000	
31.3.16 Car		8,000		
2.6.16 Machinery	31,000			
Disposals				
29.3.16 Machinery		(3,000)		
	54,800			
AIA (note)	(54,800)			54,800
		43,500		
WDA @ 18%		(7,830)		7,830
WDA @ 18%			(3,240) × 80%	2,592
c/f		35,670	14,760	
Allowances				65,222

Note. Maximum AIA = (6/12 x £500,000) + (6/12 x £200,000) = £350,000

Task 3.3

	AIA £	FYA @ 100% £	Main pool £	Allowances £
Y/e 31 March 2017				
Additions				
6.5.16 Machinery	218,250			
6.7.16 Low emission car		8,000		
31.8.16 Car			10,500	
AIA (max)	(200,000)			200,000
	18,250			
Transfer to main pool	(18,250)		18,250	
			28,750	
FYA @ 100%		(8,000)		8,000
		–		
WDA @ 18%			(5,175)	5,175
c/f			23,575	
Total allowances				213,175

Task 3.4

	Main pool £	Car (1) @ 70% £	Special rate pool £	Car (2) @ 70% £	Allowances £
Y/e 30 September 2016					
b/f	120,000	21,000	17,500		
Additions					
10.8.16 Car				25,000	
Disposal					
10.8.16 Car		(16,000)			
Balancing allowance		5,000 × 70%			3,500
WDA @ 18%	(21,600)				21,600
WDA @ 8%			(1,400)		1,400
WDA @ 8%				(2,000) × 70%	1,400
c/f	98,400		16,100	23,000	
Allowances					27,900

Task 3.5

	Main pool £	Special rate pool £	Allowances £
Y/e 31 March 2017			
b/f	106,000		
Addition		14,000	
WDA @ 18%	(19,080)		19,080
WDA @ 8%		(1,120)	1,120
c/f	86,920	12,880	
Allowances			20,200

Chapter 4 Computing corporation tax

Task 4.1

	£	£
Profit per accounts		656,980
	Add	Deduct
Depreciation charge	83,420	0
Qualifying charitable donation	1,900	0
Donation to local charity	0	0
Gifts to customers	900	0
Accountancy and audit fee	0	0
Legal fees – renewal of 20 year lease (N1)	0	0
Legal fees – issue of debenture	0	0
Repairs – knocked down wall (N2)	0	0
Initial repairs to office	12,200	0
Other expenses	0	0
Debenture interest	0	(24,700)
Bank interest	0	(4,800)
Dividends	0	(56,000)
Capital allowances	0	(13,200)
Interest payable on trading loans	0	0
Net adjustments		(280)
Taxable trading profit		656,700

Notes

1 The costs of renewing a short lease and of obtaining loan finance for trading purposes are allowable.

2 The replacement of the wall is allowable since the whole structure is not being replaced. The repairs to the office building are not allowable, being capital in nature, as the building was not in a usable state when purchased and this was reflected in the purchase price.

Task 4.2

	Allow ✓	Disallow And add back ✓	Not taxable as trading income so deduct ✓
Dividends received from an unconnected company			✓
Profit on sale of shares			✓
Running costs of car with 20% private use by an employee	✓		
Parking fine of director		✓	
Capital allowances	✓		
Director's salary	✓		
Bank interest received			✓

Task 4.3

	Year to 31 December 2016 £	Five months to 31 May 2017 £
Trading profits (12:5)	352,941	147,059
Property business income (12:5)	10,800	4,500
Chargeable gain	0	3,000
Total profits	363,741	154,559
Qualifying charitable donations paid	(30,000)	(40,000)
Taxable total profits	333,741	114,559

Tutor's notes

1 Trading profits are time apportioned.
2 Property business income is time apportioned.
3 Chargeable gains are allocated to the period in which they are realised.
4 Qualifying charitable donations are allocated to the period in which they are paid.

Task 4.4

	Time apportioned ✓	Period in which arises ✓	Separate computation ✓
Capital allowances			✓
Trading income	✓		
Property income	✓		
Interest income		✓	
Chargeable gain		✓	

Task 4.5

The corporation tax payable by Rosemary Ltd for period ended 31 March 2017 is:

£	180,000

Working:

	£
Trading profits	600,000
Property business income	300,000
Taxable total profits	900,000

Note. Dividends are not included as part of taxable total profits.

FY16	£
£900,000 × 20%	180,000

Task 4.6

Total turnover (box 145):	£525,000
Taxable trading profits (box 155):	£394,000
Net trading profits (box 165):	£394,000
Interest (box 170):	£3,000
Property business income (box 190):	£16,000
Profits (box 235):	£413,000

Chapter 5 Taxing unincorporated businesses

Task 5.1

Her first tax year is:

2014/15

Her taxable profits in her first year of trading are:

£	6,188

Her taxable profits in her second year of trading are:

£	24,750

Her taxable profits in her third tax year of trading are:

£	24,750

Overlap profits are:

£	22,688

Working:

Taxable profits

Tax year	Basis period	Taxable profits £
2014/15	(1.1.15 – 5.4.15) £33,000 × $^{3}/_{16}$ =	**6,188**
2015/16	(6.4.15 – 5.4.16) £33,000 × $^{12}/_{16}$ =	**24,750**
2016/17	(1.5.15 – 30.4.16) £33,000 × $^{12}/_{16}$ =	**24,750**

Overlap profits

The profits taxed twice are those for the period 1 May 2015 to 5 April 2016:

$^{11}/_{16}$ × £33,000

Task 5.2

Mr Phone's basis period for 2014/15 runs from:

01/07/2014

to:

05/04/2015

Mr Phone's basis period for 2015/16 runs from:

01/07/2014

to:

30/06/2015

His taxable profits in his second tax year of trading are:

£	23,500

Overlap profits are:

£	19,500

Working:

Tax year	Basis period	Taxable profits £
2014/15	Actual	
	1 July 2014 to 5 April 2015	
	(9/11 × £22,000)	18,000
2014/15	First 12 months	
	1 July 2014 to 30 June 2015	
	£22,000 + (1/12 × £18,000)	23,500
2015/16	(CYB)	
	Year ended 31 May 2016	18,000

	£
Overlap period is 1 July 2014 to 5 April 2015	18,000
and 1 June 2015 to 30 June 2015	
(1/12 × £18,000)	1,500
	19,500

Task 5.3

Mr Mug's final tax year is:

2016/17

Mr Mug's penultimate tax year is:

2015/16

His taxable profits in his final tax year of trading are:

£ 11,000

Working:

		£
2016/17	1 May 2015 to 31 December 2016 (16,000 + 4,000)	20,000
	Less overlap relief	(9,000)
		11,000

Note. Year ended 30 April 2015 was assessed in 2015/16.

Task 5.4

Jackie's first tax year is:

2012/13

Her taxable profits in her first tax year of trading are:

£	13,200

Jackie's second tax year is:

2013/14

Her taxable profits in her second tax year of trading are:

£	14,400

Jackie's final tax year is:

2016/17

Her taxable profits in her final tax year of trading are:

£	300

Over the life of her business Jackie is assessed on total profits of:

£	48,240

Working:

Tax year	Basis period	Taxable profits £
2012/13	First year – 1.5.12 to 5.4.13	
	11/15 × £18,000	13,200
2013/14	Second year 12 months to 31.7.13 (1.8.12 – 31.7.13)	
	12/15 × £18,000	14,400
2014/15	Third year y/e 31.7.14	11,700
2015/16	y/e 31.7.15	8,640
2016/17		

Tax year	Basis period	Taxable profits £
	Y/e 31.7.16	4,800
	P/e 28.2.17	5,100
		9,900
	Less overlap profits	(9,600)
		300

Overlap profits

Overlap period is 1 August 2012 to 5 April 2013, ie 8/15 × £18,000 = £9,600

Task 5.5

The year of change for Matilda's business is:

15/16

Her basis period for the tax year 14/15 is:

1/4/14 – 31/3/15

Her basis period for the tax year 15/16 is:

1/1/15 – 31/12/15

Her basis period for the tax year 16/17 is:

1/1/16- 31/12/16

Chapter 6 Partnerships

Task 6.1

	Total £	Fimbo £	Florrie £	Pom £
12 months to 31 December 2015				
Salary	5,000	5,000	0	0
Share of profits	5,000	3,000	2,000	0
Total for year	10,000	8,000	2,000	0
12 months to 31 December 2016				
Salary	5,000	5,000	0	0
Share of profits	15,000	9,000	6,000	0
Total for year	20,000	14,000	6,000	0
12 months to 31 December 2017				
Salary	6,500	6,500	0	0
Share of profits	18,500	6,167	6,167	6,166
Total for year	25,000	12,667	6,167	6,166

Task 6.2

(a)

	Total £	John £	Paul £	George £
Period ended 31 July 2014				
Division of profits	24,300	9,720	7,290	7,290
Year ended 31 July 2015				
Division of profits	16,200	6,480	4,860	4,860
Year ended 31 July 2016				
Division of profits	14,900	5,960	4,470	4,470

(b)

	John £	Paul £	George £
2013/14	4,166	3,124	3,124
2014/15	12,420	9,315	9,315
2015/16	6,480	4,860	4,860
2016/17	5,960	4,470	4,470

Working:

	John £	Paul £	George £
2013/14			
1 January 2014 – 5 April 2014			
3/7 × £(9,720/7,290/7,290)	4,166	3,124	3,124
2014/15			
(1 January 2014 to 31 December 2014)			
1 January 2014 to 31 July 2014	9,720	7,290	7,290
1 August 2014 to 31 December 2014			
5/12 × £(6,480/4,860/4,860)	2,700	2,025	2,025
	12,420	9,315	9,315
2015/16			
Year ended 31 July 2015	6,480	4,860	4,860
2016/17			
Year ended 31 July 2016	5,960	4,470	4,470

Task 6.3

Year ended 31 December 2016	Total £	Strange £	Pavin £	Lehman £
To 31 July 2016				
Salaries (15,000/5000 × 7/12)	11,667	8,750	2,917	0
Interest on capital (20,000/10,000 × 5% × 7/12)	875	583	292	0
Division of profits (48,000 × 7/12 – 11,667 – 875)	15,458	7,729	5,153	2,576
To 31 December 2016				
Salary (20,000 × 5/12)	8,333	8,333	0	0
Division of profits (48,000 × 5/12 – 8,333)	11,667	4,667	4,667	2,333
Total for year ended 31 December 2016	48,000	30,062	13,029	4,909

Task 6.4

Year ended 31 May 2016	Total £	Bob £	Annie £	John £
To 31 January 2016				
Salaries	30,000	10,000	10,000	10,000
Division of profits	30,000	15,000	7,500	7,500
To 31 May 2016				
Salaries	10,000	0	5,000	5,000
Division of profits	20,000	0	10,000	10,000
Total for year ended 31 May 2016	90,000	25,000	32,500	32,500

Task 6.5

Page 6	
Box 1	01/01/16
Box 2	31/12/16
Box 3	Retail – designer dresses
Box 11	36,000
Box 22	8,000
Box 6	Anne Curtis
Box 11	18,000
Box 22	4,000

Working:

Tax adjusted trading profit for the partnership is:

	£
Revenue	125,000
Cost of goods	(75,000)
Rental	(12,000)
Admin	(1,700)
Accountancy	(650)
Goods for own use	1,550
AIA on sewing machine	(1,200)
	36,000

Chapter 7 National insurance

Task 7.1

The Class 2 NIC liability for 2016/17 is:

£	145	.	60

The Class 4 NIC liability for 2016/17 is:

£	429	.	30

The total NIC liability for 2016/17 is:

£	574	.	90

Working:

	£
Profits	12,830
Less lower profits limit	(8,060)
Excess	4,770

Class 4 NICs (9% × £4,770) = £429.30

Class 2 NICs = £2.80 × 52 = £145.60

Total NICs £(429.30 + 145.60) = **£574.90**

Task 7.2

The Class 2 NIC liability for 2016/17 is:

£	145	.	60

The Class 4 NIC liability for 2016/17 is:

£	3,244	.	60

The total NIC liability for 2016/17 is:

£	3,390	.	20

Working:

	£
Upper profits limit	43,000
Less: lower profits limit	(8,060)
Excess	34,940

	£
Class 4 NICs (9% × £34,940)	3,144.60
+ 2% × £(48,000 – 43,000)	100.00
	3,244.60

Class 2 NICs = £2.80 × 52 = £145.60

Total NICs £(3,244.60 + 145.60) = **£3,390.20**

Task 7.3

The Class 2 NIC liability for 2016/17 is:

£	0	.	0

The Class 4 NIC liability for 2016/17 is:

£	0	.	0

The total NIC liability for 2016/17 is:

£	0	.	0

As Raj's trading profits are below the lower profits limit, there is no liability to Class 4 NICs. There is also no liability to Class 2 NICs because his profits are below the small profits threshold of £5,965.

Task 7.4

The Class 2 NIC liability for 2016/17 is:

£	145	.	60

The Class 4 NIC liability for 2016/17 is:

£	3,884	.	60

The total NIC liability for 2016/17 is:

£	4,030	.	20

Working:

Class 2 = £2.80 × 52 = £145.60

		£
Class 4	£(43,000 – 8,060) × 9% (main)	3,144.60
	£(80,000 – 43,000) × 2% (additional)	740.00
		3,884.60

Total NICs £(3,884.60 + 145.60) = **£4,030.20**

Task 7.5

(a) The share of profits taxable on Paula for 2016/17 is:

£	9,000

Working:

Share of profits for y/e 31.12.17 is £180,000 × 20% = £36,000
Basis period for 2016/17 = 1.1.17 to 5.4.17 (3/12 × £36,000 = £9,000)

and for 2017/18 is:

£	36,000

Working:

Basis period for 2017/18 = 1.1.17 to 31.12.17

and the overlap profits to carry forward are:

£	9,000

Working:

1.1.17 to 5.4.17 (3/12 × £36,000 = £9,000)

(b) The Class 4 National Insurance Contributions payable by Paula for 2016/17 are:

£	84	.	60

Working:

£(9,000 – 8,060) = £940 × 9%

Chapter 8 Losses

Task 8.1

	2014/15 £	2015/16 £	2016/17 £	2017/18 £
Trading profits	12,000	0	8,000	14,000
Trading loss offset against future year	0	0	(8,000)	(3,600)
Property income	10,400	11,000	11,000	11,000
Trading loss offset against current year	0	(11,000)	0	0
Trading loss offset against previous year	(22,400)	0	0	0
Net income	0	0	11,000	21,400

Task 8.2

	✓
True	
False	✓

An individual cannot restrict a claim to set a trading loss against total income in order to have enough net income to use his personal allowance – the loss must be set-off as far as possible even if this means that the personal allowance is not available.

Task 8.3

	✓
True	
False	✓

An individual does not have to make a trading loss claim against total income in the tax year of the loss before making a claim to set the loss against total income in the preceding year – a claim can be made for either year or both years, and in any order.

Task 8.4

	✓
True	✓
False	

An individual can only carry a trading loss forward against trading income of the same trade.

Task 8.5

(a)

	Year ended 30 June		
	2014	**2015**	**2016**
Trading profits	62,000	20,000	0
Interest	1,200	600	1,200
Total profits	63,200	20,600	1,200
Current period loss relief	0	0	(1,200)
Carry back loss relief	0	(20,600)	0
Total profits after loss relief	63,200	0	0
Qualifying charitable donation	(100)	0	0
Taxable total profits	63,100	0	0

(b) The trading loss available to carry forward at 30 June 2016 is:

£	61,200

Working:

(£83,000 – £1,200 – £20,600)

Task 8.6

(a)

	Year ended 30.9.14	9 months to 30.6.15	Year ended 30.6.16	Year ended 30.6.17
Trading profits	6,200	4,320	0	53,000
Carry forward loss relief	0	0	0	(53,000)
Interest	80	240	260	200
Property income	1,420	1,440	1,600	1,500
Chargeable gains	0	7,680	0	0
Total profits	7,700	13,680	1,860	1,700
Current period loss relief	0	0	(1,860)	0
Carry back loss relief	(1,925)	(13,680)	0	0
Total profits after loss relief	5,775	0	0	1,700
Qualifying charitable donation	(1,000)	0	0	(1,500)
Taxable total profits	4,775	0	0	200

Tutor's note. The loss can be carried back to set against profits arising in the previous 12 months. This means that the set-off in the y/e 30.9.14 is restricted to 3/12 × £7,700 = £1,925.

(b) The trading loss available to carry forward at 30 June 2017 is:

£	29,535

Working:

(£100,000 – £1,860 – £13,680 – £1,925 – £53,000)

(c) The capital loss available to carry forward at 30 June 2017 is:

£	9,423

Task 8.7

	✓
True	✓
False	

A company must offset its trading loss against total profits in the loss-making period before carrying the loss back.

Task 8.8

	✓
True	
False	✓

If a company carries a trading loss forward, the loss can only be set against trading profits from the same trade.

Task 8.9

	✓
True	
False	✓

A company can set-off a capital loss against capital gains only.

Chapter 9 Self assessment for individuals

Task 9.1

	✓
31 January 2018	✓
5 April 2018	
31 October 2017	
31 December 2017	

Task 9.2

	✓
The full amount of £20,500 will be paid on 31 January 2018.	
Payments on account based on the estimated 2016/17 liability will be made on 31 January and 31 July 2017, with the balance payable on 31 January 2018.	
Payments on account of £10,250 will be made on 31 January and 31 July 2017 with nothing due on 31 January 2018.	
Payments on account of £7,250 will be made on 31 January and 31 July 2017, with the balance of £6,000 being paid on 31 January 2018.	✓

Task 9.3

	✓
100%	
50%	✓
35%	
15%	

Task 9.4

	✓
0%	
20%	
30%	✓
35%	

Task 9.5

	✓
True	✓
False	

The return is filed less than 3 months after the due filing date.

Task 9.6

	✓
True	✓
False	

The penalty for failure to keep records is £3,000 per tax year or accounting period.

Task 9.7

	✓
True	
False	✓

Penalties for late payment do not apply to payments on account.

Chapter 10 Self assessment for companies

Task 10.1

Instalment	Due date	Amount due £
1	14/10/2016	125,000
2	14/01/2017	125,000
3	14/04/2017	125,000
4	14/07/2017	125,000

Task 10.2

	True ✓	False ✓
A company with a period of account ending on 31 March 2017 must keep its records until 31 March 2019.		✓ (until 31 March 2023)
The due date for payment of CGT for 2016/17 is 31 January 2018.	✓	
An individual who becomes chargeable to income tax in 2016/17 must notify HMRC by 31 October 2017.		✓ (by 5 October 2017)
A large company will not have to pay corporation tax by instalments if it has profits not exceeding £10m and was not large in the previous accounting period.	✓	
A company which is not large (for corporation tax purposes) must pay its corporation tax by nine months and one day after the end of its accounting period.	✓	

Task 10.3

The corporation tax return must be filed by:

28/02/18

The corporation tax return must be filed by:

30/06/2017

Task 10.4

A company must keep its accounting records for **six** years. Failure to do so may incur a penalty of £ 3,000.

Task 10.5

The fact that Fred derives nearly all of his income from one client, and uses that client's equipment implies that IR35 may apply, as they are aspects of engagement generally associated with permanent employment.

The fact that Fred can provide a replacement to perform his duties would suggest that IR35 does not apply.

Fred will be taxed on a deemed employment charge.

This will be subject to income tax and NICs.

The dividends he is currently extracting from Fred Services Ltd are not subject to NICs.

There are fewer expenses deductible from the deemed employment charge than from a company.

Task 10.6

The amount which is deductible as a trading expense is £ 115,000.

(£50,000 × 230%)

If this resulted in a loss, the loss could be surrendered in exchange for a tax credit at the rate of 14.5 %.

Chapter 11 Chargeable gains – the basics

Task 11.1

For the gain on the disposal of a capital asset to be a chargeable gain there must be a chargeable [disposal] of a chargeable [asset] by a chargeable [person].

Task 11.2

Item	Chargeable ✓	Exempt ✓
Wasting chattel with useful life of 25 years		✓
Disposal of half the holding of a plot of land	✓	
Car used for business purposes		✓

Task 11.3

	✓
£33,900	✓
£38,900	
£45,000	
£50,000	

Working:

	£
Proceeds of sale	90,000
Less cost	(40,000)
Less enhancement expenditure	(5,000)
Chargeable gain	45,000
Less annual exempt amount	(11,100)
Taxable gain	33,900

Task 11.4

(a) George's capital gains tax liability for 2016/17 is:

£	1,068

Working:

	£
Chargeable gains	20,000
Less allowable losses	(3,560)
Net chargeable gains	16,440
Less annual exempt amount	(11,100)
Taxable gains	5,340
CGT @ 20%	**£1,068**

(b) George's capital gains tax liability is payable by:

31 January 2018

Task 11.5

Jack would pay capital gains tax at:

28%

Gains on residential property are subject to capital gains tax at 18% (for basic rate taxpayer) and 28% (for higher and additional rate taxpayers).

Task 11.6

The amount of the loss Graham will use in 2016/17 is:

£	5,200

Note. Current year losses cannot be restricted in order to get the benefit of the annual exempt amount.

Working:

	£
Chargeable gains	15,000
Less allowable losses	(5,200)
Net chargeable gains	9,800
Less annual exempt amount	(11,100)
Taxable gains	0

Task 11.7

Gayle's capital gains tax liability for 2016/17 is:

£	1,380

Working:

	£
Chargeable gains	22,500
Less allowable losses	(2,000)
Net chargeable gains	20,500
Less annual exempt amount	(11,100)
Taxable gains	9,400

CGT payable

	£
£5,000 @ 10%	500
£4,400 @ 20%	880
	1,380

Task 11.8

Gerry's capital gains tax liability for 2016/17 is:

£	2,301

Working:

	£
Chargeable gains	27,100
Less annual exempt amount	(11,100)
Taxable gains	16,000

CGT	£
£8,995 (W) @ 10%	900
£7,005 @ 20%	1,401
	2,301
(W) Unused basic rate band is £32,000 – £23,005 = £8,995	

Task 11.9

The losses to carry forward to 2017/18 are:

£	3,800

Working:

(5,000 – 1,200)

	£
Gains	18,900
Losses	(6,600)
	12,300
Losses b/f (12,300 – 11,100)	(1,200)
	11,100
Less annual exempt amount	(11,100)
Taxable gains	Nil

Task 11.10

The maximum allowable loss carried forward to 2017/18 will be:

£	11,400

Working:

Tax year	2014/15 £	2015/16 £	2016/17 £
Gains	2,000	4,000	13,700
Losses	(14,000)	(2,000)	(2,000)
Net gain/(loss)	(12,000)	2,000	11,700
Less loss b/f	(0)	0	(600)
Less annual exempt amount	0	(2,000)	(11,100)
Chargeable gain	0	0	0
Loss c/f	(12,000)	(12,000)	(11,400)

The use of the loss brought forward in 2016/17 is restricted to the amount of the annual exempt amount.

Task 11.11

	£
Proceeds	230,000
Less cost	(160,000)
Unindexed gain	70,000
Less indexation allowance 0.514 × £160,000 (restricted)	(70,000)
Chargeable gain/allowable loss	0

Task 11.12

	£
Proceeds	180,000
Less: cost	(100,000)
enhancement expenditure	(25,000)
Unindexed gain	55,000
Less: indexation allowance on cost 0.345 × £100,000	(34,500)
indexation allowance on enhancement 0.246 × £25,000	(6,150)
Chargeable gain	14,350

Task 11.13

	✓
True	
False	✓

Individuals are entitled to an annual exempt amount but not companies.

Chapter 12 Further aspects of chargeable gains

Task 12.1

(a) The cost of the land sold is:

£	120,000

Working:

$$\frac{240,000}{240,000+60,000} \times £150,000$$

(b) The gain on sale is:

£	117,000

Working:

	£
Disposal proceeds	240,000
Less: disposal costs	(3,000)
Net proceeds	237,000
Less: cost	(120,000)
Chargeable gain	**117,000**

Task 12.2

Her chargeable gain on sale is:

	✓
£2,300	
£2,000	
£2,500	
£1,700	✓

Working:

	£
Gross proceeds	7,500
Less: costs of sale	(300)
Net proceeds	7,200
Less: cost	(5,500)
Chargeable gain	1,700
Gain cannot exceed 5/3 × £(7,500 – 6,000)	2,500

Task 12.3

Mark's allowable loss is:

£	3,500

Working:

	£
Deemed proceeds	6,000
Less: costs of sale £(4,500 × 100/90) = £5,000 × 10%	(500)
Net proceeds	5,500
Less: cost	(9,000)
Allowable loss	**(3,500)**

Task 12.4

	✓
True	
False	✓

The proceeds are less than £6,000 so the gain is exempt.

Task 12.5

John's chargeable gains (before the annual exempt amount) for 2016/17 are:

	✓
£45,000	✓
£30,000	
£34,100	
£19,100	

The gain on the disposal to John's brother is £(60,000 – 15,000) = £45,000. The loss on the disposal to John's daughter can only be set against disposals to that connected person.

Task 12.6

	✓
True	✓
False	

Disposals to connected persons are deemed to be at market value.

Task 12.7

(a) The cost of the two offices disposed of is:

£	76,087

Working:

$$£250,000 \times \frac{140,000}{140,000 + 320,000}$$

(b) The chargeable gain arising on the disposal is:

£	28,304

Working:

	£
Proceeds	140,000
Less: cost	(76,087)
	63,913
Less: IA	
0.468 × £76,087	(35,609)
Chargeable gain	**28,304**

Task 12.8

	£
Proceeds	8,000
Disposal costs	(500)
Cost of acquisition	(4,500)
Indexation allowance (4,500 × 0.238)	(1,071)
Gain	1,929
Gain using chattel marginal relief 5/3 (8,000 – 6,000)	3,333
Chargeable gain (lower of actual gain and marginal relief)	1,929

Chapter 13 Share disposals

Task 13.1

His net gain on sale is:

£	9,800

Working:

Match acquisition in next 30 days first

	£
Proceeds of sale £20,000 × 1,000/5,000	4,000
Less: cost	(4,200)
Loss	(200)

Then match with share pool

	£
Proceeds of sale £20,000 × 4,000/5,000	16,000
Less: cost £9,000 × 4,000/6,000	(6,000)
Gain	10,000

Task 13.2

Share pool

	No. of shares	Cost £
10 February 2001	12,000	18,000
20 September 2008 Bonus 1:4	3,000	0
Total before disposal	15,000	18,000
15 March 2017 Disposal	(2,000)	(2,400)
c/f	13,000	15,600

Gain on sale

	£
Proceeds	8,000
Less: cost	(2,400)
Gain	5,600

Task 13.3

Share pool

	No. of shares	Cost £
9 December 2001: purchase	12,000	4,400
12 October 2005 Rights 1:3@ £5	4,000	20,000
Total before disposal	16,000	24,400
4 November 2016 Disposal	(8,000)	(12,200)
c/f	8,000	12,200

Gains on sale

	£	£
Next 30 days		
Proceeds (2,000/10,000 × 60,000)	12,000	
Cost	(11,500)	
Gain/(loss)		500
Share pool		
Proceeds (8,000/10,000 × 60,000)	48,000	
Cost	(12,200)	
Gain/(loss)		35,800
Total gain/(loss)		36,300

Task 13.4

FA 1985 pool

	No. of shares	Original cost £	Indexed cost £
September 2001			
Acquisition	5,000	10,000	10,000
October 2004			
Indexed rise 0.080 × £10,000			800
Rights 1:5 @ £5	1,000	5,000	5,000
	6,000	15,000	15,800
August 2006			
Indexed rise 0.056 × £15,800			885
Acquisition	14,000	84,000	84,000
	20,000	99,000	100,685
January 2017			
Indexed rise 0.323 × £100,685			32,521
			133,206
Sale (99,000/133,206 × 18,000/20,000)	(18,000)	(89,100)	(119885)
c/f	2,000	9,900	13,321

Gain

	£
Proceeds	155,000
Less: cost	(89,100)
	65,900
Less: indexation allowance £(119,885 – 89,100)	(30,785)
Chargeable gain	35,115

Task 13.5

FA 1985 pool

	No. of shares	Cost £	Indexed cost £
26 May 1995			
Acquisition	4,000	24,000	24,000
30 June 1996 Bonus issue (1/2 × 4,000)	2,000		
24 October 2003			
Indexed rise 0.221 × £24,000			5,304
Acquisition	5,000	27,500	27,500
c/f	11,000	51,500	56,804
25 May 2016			
Indexed rise 0.428 × £56,804			24,312
			81,116
Disposal	(11,000)	(51,500)	(81,116)
c/f	0	0	0

Gain

	£
Proceeds	78,200
Less cost	(51,500)
	26,700
Less indexation allowance £(81,116 – 51,500)	(29,616)
Gain	Nil

Task 13.6

	✓
True	✓
False	

Indexation allowance on rights issue shares runs from the date of the rights issue even though the rights issue shares are treated as having been acquired at the time of the original acquisition to which they relate.

Chapter 14 Reliefs for chargeable gains

Task 14.1

	£	£
Proceeds of goodwill	50,000	
Less cost	0	
Gain/(loss) on goodwill		50,000
Proceeds of shop	90,000	
Less cost	(80,000)	
Gain/(loss) on shop		10,000
Proceeds of warehouse	130,000	
Less cost	(150,000)	
Gain/(loss) on warehouse		(20,000)
Net gains eligible for entrepreneurs' relief		40,000
Less annual exempt amount		(11,100)
Taxable gains		28,900
CGT payable		2,890

Task 14.2

	✓
True	✓
False	

The lifetime limit of gains eligible for entrepreneurs' relief is £10,000,000.

Task 14.3

The taxable gain arising on the sale of the Blue Ltd shares is:

£	138,900

Working:

	£	£
Proceeds		200,000
Less cost	65,000	
Less gain rolled over	(15,000)	
		(50,000)
Chargeable gain		150,000
Less annual exempt amount		(11,100)
Taxable gain		**138,900**

Task 14.4

(a) Fran's chargeable gain on her disposal is:

£	0

Working:

	£
Proceeds (MV) June 2016	500,000
Less cost	(75,000)
Gain	425,000
Less gift relief	(425,000)
Gain left in charge	**0**

(b) Anna's chargeable gain on her disposal is:

£	445,000

Working:

	£	£
Proceeds July 2017		520,000
Cost (MV)	500,000	
Less gift relief gain (from above)	(425,000)	
Base cost		(75,000)
Chargeable gain		**445,000**

Task 14.5

(a) Edward's gain on the disposal before rollover relief is:

£	65,000

Working:

	£
Proceeds	125,000
Less cost	(60,000)
Gain	**65,000**

(b) Assuming rollover relief is claimed, the gain immediately chargeable is:

£	1,500

Proceeds not re-invested (£125,000 – £123,500)

(c) The gain which Edward can rollover into the new premises is:

£	£63,500

Working:

	£
Gain	65,000
Less immediately chargeable	(1,500)
Gain rolled-over against new premises	63,500

Task 14.6

(a) The gain on disposal in May 2013 was:

£	73,250

Working:

	£
Proceeds	145,000
Less cost	(50,000)
	95,000
Less indexation allowance 0.435 × £50,000	(21,750)
Chargeable gain	**73,250**

(b) The gain available for rollover relief is:

£	68,250

Working:

	£
Gain	73,250
Less chargeable in 2013	
Proceeds not reinvested = £(145,000 – 140,000)	(5,000)
Gain available for rollover relief	**68,250**

(c) The base cost of the property acquired in April 2016 is:

£	71,750

Working:

	£
Cost of new property	140,000
Less gain rolled over	(68,250)
Base cost of new property	**71,750**

Task 14.7

	✓
The start of the previous accounting period and the end of the next accounting period	
Three years before and three years after the date of the disposal	
One year before and three years after the date of the disposal	✓
One year before and one year after the date of the disposal	

AAT AQ2016 SAMPLE ASSESSMENT 1

Business Tax

Time allowed: 2 hours

AAT AQ2016 SAMPLE ASSESMENT 1

BPP LEARNING MEDIA

Business Tax (BSTX)
AAT sample assessment 1

Task 1 (10 marks)

(a) In relation to the computation of taxable trading profits, link the following items to the correct treatment. (3 marks)

(CBT instructions: *In relation to the computation of taxable trading profits, link the following items to the correct treatment by clicking on the left-hand box and then the appropriate right-hand box. You can remove a line by clicking on it.*)

Item	Treatment
General provision for irrecoverable debts	
Donation of £1,000 to a political party	Disallow and deduct
Bottles of whisky, each costing £45, with the company logo on the side, given free to customers	Disallow and add back
Gain on sale of shares	Allow
Repairs to factory floors	
Profit on sales of a lorry	

Meredith started trading on 1 February 2015 making up her first set of accounts for the 15-month period to 30 April 2016. Her adjusted trading profits were agreed as:

Period ended 30 April 2016: £94,920
Year ended 30 April 2017: £61,980

(b) Show the taxable profits for the second and third tax years in the table below. Complete the dates for the basis periods by selecting a day from each calendar window and entering the year in the format YYYY (eg 2016) in the adjoining boxes.

(6 marks)

Taxable year	Basis period start	Basis period end	Profit £
▼			
▼			

Drop-down list:

2012/2013
2013/2014
2014/2015
2015/2016
2016/2017
2017/2018

(c) Complete the following statement: **(1 mark)**

Meredith has overlap profits of £ [ ]

Task 2 (10 marks)

Chris and Pat are in partnership, trading as estate agents, with an accounting year end of 31 March. They shared profits 3:1 respectively. On 1 August 2016 they started to take a salary and shared profits 65% and 35% respectively. From 1 August 2016 they also started to receive interest on capital introduced into the business. Their salaries and contributed capital are shown below.

	Chris	Pat
Salary per year	£9,000	£4,500
Capital introduced	£15,000	£6,000
Interest on capital	3%	2%

The taxable profit for the year ended 31 March 2017 was £71,460.

(a) Show the division of profit for the year ended 31 March 2017. If your answer is zero, enter 0. Round your answer to the nearest pound if appropriate. (8 marks)

To 31 July 2016	Chris £	Pat £
Share of profits		

From 1 August 2016	Chris £	Pat £
Interest on capital		
Salary		
Share of profits		

(b) Calculate Pat's National Insurance contributions (NIC) for 2016/17.

Your answer should be to the nearest penny. If your answer is zero, enter 0. (2 marks)

NIC	Pat Amount payable £
Class 2	
Class 4 at 9%	
Class 4 at 2%	

Task 3 (13 marks)

Arthur runs a painting and decorating business as a sole trader. He has the following fixed asset information for the 15-month period ended 31 March 2017:

Balances brought forward as at 1 January 2016	£
General pool	58,995
Arthur's car: CO2 emissions of 110 g/km 25% private use	18,850

Additions	£
17 April 2016, Arthur's car: CO_2 emissions of 75 g/km 15% private use	29,750
22 February 2017, 10 vans	236,050

Disposals	£
15 April 2016, Arthur's car: CO_2 emissions of 110 g/km 25% private use	12,850
25 February 2017, 10 vans originally purchased in 2013	34,000

(a) Calculate the maximum Annual Investment Allowance that Arthur can claim for the period ended 31 March 2017.

(2 marks)

(b) Calculate the capital allowances that Arthur can claim for the period ended 31 March 2017. (11 marks)

Task 4 (6 marks)

In the table below is the information needed for Destine Ltd to complete its corporation tax return for the year ended 31 December 2016.

	£
Turnover	1,400,250
Trading profits	500,350
Trading losses brought forward	650,250
Net rental income	85,750
Chargeable gains	28,890

Complete the relevant boxes on the following extract from Destine Ltd's corporation tax return for the year ended 31 December 2016.
(6 marks)

Tax calculation

Turnover

145	**Total turnover from trade**	£
150	**Banks, building societies, insurance companies and other financial concerns -** *put an 'X' in this box if you do not have a recognised turnover and have not made an entry in box 145*	

Income

155	**Trading profits**	£
160	**Trading losses brought forward claimed against profits**	£
165	**Net trading profits -** *box 155 minus box 160*	£
170	**Bank, building society or other interest, and profits from non-trading loan relationships**	£
172	**Put an 'X' in box 172 if the figure in box 170 is net of carrying back a deficit from a later accounting period**	
175	**Annual payments not otherwise charged to Corporation Tax and from which Income Tax has not been deducted**	£

Income *continued*

180	Non-exempt dividends or distributions from non-UK resident companies	£	
185	Income from which Income Tax has been deducted	£	
190	Income from a property business	£	
195	Non-trading gains on intangible fixed assets	£	
200	Tonnage Tax profits	£	
205	Income not falling under any other heading	£	

Chargeable gains

210	Gross chargeable gains	£	
215	Allowable losses including losses brought forward	£	
220	Net chargeable gains - *box 210 minus box 215*	£	

Profits before deductions and reliefs

225	Losses brought forward against certain investment income	£	
230	Non-trade deficits on loan relationships (including interest) and derivative contracts (financial instruments) brought forward	£	
235	Profits before other deductions and reliefs - *net sum of boxes 165 to 205 and 220 minus sum of boxes 225 and 230*	£	

Task 5 (9 marks)

Faversham Ltd has prepared accounts for the 15-month period ended 31 December 2016. Taxable profits and charges for the period are shown in the table below.

Taxable profit or charge	Amount £
Trading profit	238,350
Bank interest received on 1 May 2016	3,525
Rental income received throughout period	12,750
Gift aid donation made on 14 November 2016	5,200

(a) Calculate the apportionment of the taxable profits and charges between the two accounting periods for the period of account to 31 December 2016. You should round your answers to the nearest whole pound where appropriate. If your answer is zero, enter 0. (6 marks)

Taxable profit or charge	Accounting period ended 30 September 2016 £	Accounting period ended 31 December 2016 £
Trading profit		
Bank interest		
Rental income		
Gift aid donation		

(b) Calculate the corporation tax payable by Faversham Ltd for the two accounting periods. You should round your answers to the nearest whole pound where appropriate. (2 marks)

	Accounting period ended 30 September 2016 £	Accounting period ended 31 December 2016 £
Corporation tax payable		

Whitstable Ltd is a trading company and had an accounting loss for the year ended 31 January 2017 of £(48,950).

The loss was calculated after a depreciation charge for the year of £12,750.

(c) Calculate Whitstable Ltd's taxable trading loss for the year ended 31 January 2017. Do not use brackets or minus signs. (1 mark)

	Year ended 31 January 2017 £
Taxable trading loss	

Task 6 (7 marks)

Margi has been trading for a number of years and her liability to Income Tax and Class 4 NI is as follows:

2013/2014 £3678
2014/2015 £4856
2015/2016 £5860

(a) Complete the following payment schedule, showing dates and amounts due, that Margi will pay in the calendar year 2017. Complete the dates for the basis periods by selecting a day from each calendar window and entering the year in the format YYYY (eg 2017) in the adjoining boxes. (6 marks)

Taxable year	Payment day	Payment year	Payment type	Amount £
▼			▼	
▼			▼	
▼			▼	

Drop-down list:

2012/2013
2013/2014
2014/2015
2015/2016
2016/2017
2017/2018
Balancing payment
First payment on account
Second payment on account

Greyston Ltd has an accounting year end of 31 March 2017.

(b) Complete the following sentence. **(1 mark)**

The latest date for filing its CT600 corporation tax return is [▼]

Drop-down list:

5 April 2017
31 January 2018
31 March 2018
5 April 2018

Task 7 (8 marks)

(a) Identify whether the following statements are true or false:

(6 marks)

Statement	True ✓	False ✓
An individual who files a paper self assessment return on 25 January following the end of the tax year will incur a penalty of £100.		
An individual may amend a self assessment return up to one year after the submission date, provided it was not filed late.		
Charlie's accountant has found an error in Charlie's 2014 self assessment return. If Charlie admits the error to HMRC, it would be considered an unprompted error.		
Late payment penalties are only payable for late payment of balancing payments, not payments on account.		
To avoid a penalty, a company that commenced trading on 1 September 2016 should notify HMRC it is within the scope of corporation tax by 5 April 2017.		
If a company submits a CT600 for the accounting year ended 31 December 2016 on 31 August 2017, HMRC must notify the company of an enquiry by 31 December 2018.		

Suzie has made an unprompted disclosure to the Inland Revenue. It was considered a deliberate but not concealed error and has resulted in further tax payable of £2,000.

(b) Complete the following sentence. **(2 marks)**

She will incur a minimum penalty of | £ | | and a maximum penalty of | £ | |.

Task 8 (5 marks)

The following statements are about how trading losses of a company can be utilised.

Identify whether the following statements are true or false.

(5 marks)

Statement	True ✓	False ✓
Trading losses can be carried forward and offset against future chargeable gains.		
Trading losses can be carried back to be utilised in any of the previous three years.		
Trading losses can be offset against current year chargeable gains.		
Carrying forward trading losses is the most advantageous option for cash flow.		
Trading losses carried forward can only be used in the next accounting period.		
Trading losses must first be offset against current year total profits before being carried back to a previous period.		
Trading losses are offset against total profits in priority to Gift Aid donations.		

Task 9 (14 marks)

You work for a firm of accountants and the following email has been received from a client.

From: jason@jpit.com

To: post@fpaccounting.com

Through my limited company. I have recently started working full time as an IT consultant for a large retail distributor. My contract with the company requires me to provide my services exclusively, although I am able to provide a replacement consultant when off sick or on holiday. My company charges the client a monthly fee of £6,000.

I provide the services from my office at home and use all of my company's IT equipment in providing the services. You may recall my company purchased this equipment for £20,000 a few years ago.

A friend has mentioned that there is legislation called IR35 that might affect how the income from this work is treated for tax purposes. Up to now my company has been paying me a monthly salary of £1,000 with any residual profits drawn as dividends.

I would be grateful if you could reply with some further information. If you have any other clients in a similar position to me could you send me a copy of their tax return?

Thanks, Jason.

In the spaces provided below prepare notes to help with the writing of a reply to Jason's email.

(a) Briefly summarise the intermediaries (IR35) legislation.

(3 marks)

(b) An explanation of how income is taxed differently under IR35 legislation compared to how Jason's income from the company is currently taxed. (3 marks)

(c) Explain which aspects of the work suggest IR35 may apply and which suggest IR35 may NOT apply. (7 marks)

(d) Reply to Jason's request for information regarding other clients' tax returns. (1 mark)

Task 10 (8 marks)

Le Bon Ltd sold two assets during December 2016 – a painting and an antique bookcase. The painting was bought in June 2004 for £38,700 and sold in December 2016 for £62,450

During the period of ownership, Le Bon Ltd had spent £940 on insurance for this painting. The bookcase was bought in May 2007 for £16,650. In August 2011, Le Bon Ltd spent £1,880 repairing the wood on some of the shelves. The bookcase was sold in December 2016 for £31,650.

The indexation factors are shown below.

	December 2016
June 2004	0.413
May 2007	0.266
August 2011	0.096

Calculate the chargeable gain on the disposal of these assets. Do not use brackets or minus signs. (8 marks)

	Painting £	Bookcase £
Proceeds		
Total cost		
Total indexation allowance		
Gain		

Task 11 (10 marks)

Redey Ltd had the following transactions in the shares of Vinish Ltd.

Date	Event	No. of shares	£ per share
March 2010	Purchase	2500	50
April 2011	Bonus issue	1 for 5	
November 2012	Rights issue	1 for 2	45
10 October 2016	Purchase	1500	75
18 October 2016	Sale	2750	85

Relevant indexation factors are:

Month	April 2011	November 2012	October 2016
March 2010	0.062	0.113	0.187
April 2011	–	0.048	0.118
November 2012	–	–	0.067

Calculate the total chargeable gain or loss for the disposal of these shares in October 2016 and the value of the shares carried forward after the disposal. (10 marks)

AAT AQ2016 SAMPLE ASSESSMENT 1

Business Tax

ANSWERS

Business Tax (BSTX)
AAT sample assessment 1

In the live assessment you will have access to the Tax tables and reference material which have been reproduced at the back of this Question Bank (see page 241–259). Please use them whilst completing this practice assessment so that you are familiar with their content.

Task 1 (10 marks)

(a) In relation to the computation of taxable trading profits, link the following items to the correct treatment. (3 marks)

(CBT instructions: *In relation to the computation of taxable trading profits, link the following items to the correct treatment by clicking on the left-hand box and then the appropriate right-hand box. You can remove a line by clicking on it.*)

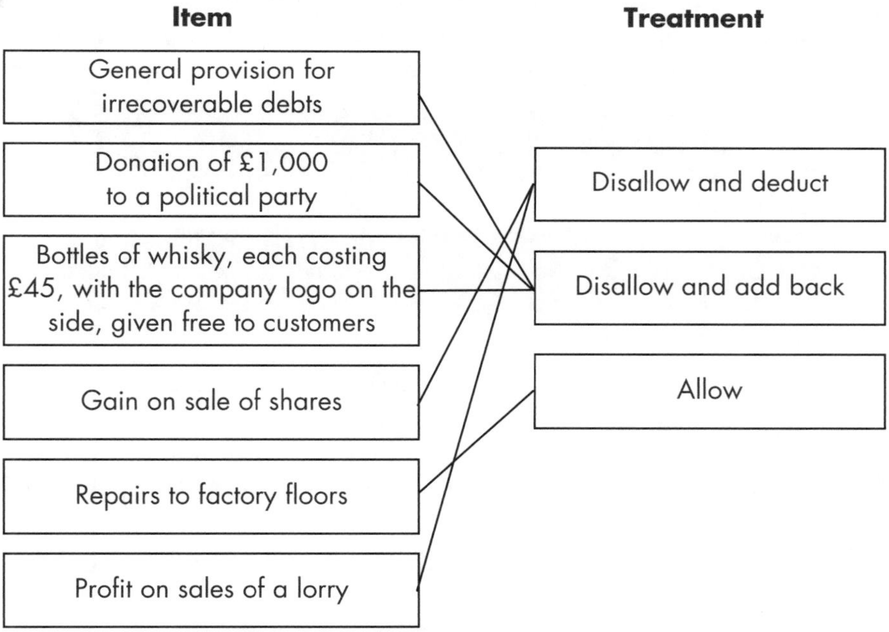

Meredith started trading on 1 February 2015 making up her first set of accounts for the 15-month period to 30 April 2016. Her adjusted trading profits were agreed as:

Period ended 30 April 2016: £94,920
Year ended 30 April 2017: £61,980

(b) Show the taxable profits for the second and third tax years in the table below. Complete the dates for the basis periods by selecting a day from each calendar window and entering the year in the format YYYY (eg 2016) in the adjoining boxes. (6 marks)

Taxable year	Basis period start	Basis period end	Profit £
2015/2016	6 April 2015	5 April 2016	75,936
2016/2017	1 May 2015	30 April 2016	75,936

(c) Complete the following statement: (1 mark)

Meredith has overlap profits of | £ | 69,608 |

Task 2 (10 marks)

(a) Show the division of profit for the year ended 31 March 2017. If your answer is zero, enter 0. Round your answer to the nearest pound if appropriate. (8 marks)

To 31 July 2016	Chris £	Pat £
Share of profits	17,865	5,955
From 1 August 2016	**Chris £**	**Pat £**
Interest on capital	300	80
Salary	6,000	3,000
Share of profits	24,869	13,391

(b) Calculate Pat's National Insurance contributions (NIC) for 2016/17.

Your answer should be to the nearest penny. If your answer is zero, enter 0. (2 marks)

NIC	Pat Amount payable £
Class 2	145.60
Class 4 at 9%	1,285.74
Class 4 at 2%	0

Task 3 (13 marks)

(a) Calculate the maximum Annual Investment Allowance that Arthur can claim for the period ended 31 March 2017.

(2 marks)

15/12 × £200,000 = £250,000

(b) Calculate the capital allowances that Arthur can claim for the period ended 31 March 2017. **(11 marks)**

	AIA/FYA	General Pool	Arthur's car (25%)	Allowances
B'fwd		58,995	18,850	
Additions				
10 vans	236,050			
AIA	(236,050)			236,050
Disposals				
10 vans		(34,000)		
Arthur's car			(12,850)	
		24,995	6,000	
Balancing allowance			(6,000)	4,500
WDA at 18% 15 months		(5,624)		5,624
Addition				
Arthur's new car	29,750			
FYA	(29,750)			× 85% = 25,288
Total capital allowances				271,462
C'fwd		19,371		

Task 4 (6 marks)

Complete the relevant boxes on the following extract from Destine Ltd's corporation tax return for the year ended 31 December 2016.
(6 marks)

Box 145	£1,400,250
Box 155	£500,350
Box 160	£500,350
Box 165	£0
Box 190	£85,750
Box 210	£28,890
Box 215	£0
Box 220	£28,890
Box 235	£114,640

Task 5 (9 marks)

(a) Calculate the apportionment of the taxable profits and charges between the two accounting periods for the period of account to 31 December 2016. You should round your answers to the nearest whole pound where appropriate. If your answer is zero, enter 0. **(6 marks)**

Taxable profit or charge	Accounting period ended 30 September 2016 £	Accounting period ended 31 December 2016 £
Trading profit	190,680	47,670
Bank interest	2,820	705
Rental income	10,200	2,550
Gift aid donation	0	5,200

(b) Calculate the corporation tax payable by Faversham Ltd for the two accounting periods. You should round your answers to the nearest whole pound where appropriate. (2 marks)

	Accounting period ended 30 September 2016 £	Accounting period ended 31 December 2016 £
Corporation tax payable	40,740	9,145

Whitstable Ltd is a trading company and had an accounting loss for the year ended 31 January 2017 of £(48,950).

The loss was calculated after a depreciation charge for the year of £12,750.

(c) Calculate Whitstable Ltd's taxable trading loss for the year ended 31 January 2017. Do not use brackets or minus signs. (1 mark)

	Year ended 31 January 2017 £
Taxable trading loss	36,200

Task 6 (7 marks)

(a) Complete the following payment schedule, showing dates and amounts due, that Margi will pay in the calendar year 2017. Complete the dates for the basis periods by selecting a day from each calendar window and entering the year in the format YYYY (eg 2017) in the adjoining boxes. (6 marks)

Taxable year	Payment day	Payment year	Payment type	Amount £
2015/2016	31 January	2017	Balancing payment	1,004
2016/2017	31 January	2017	First payment on account	2,930
2016/2017	31 July	2017	Second payment on account	2,930

Greyston Ltd has an accounting year end of 31 March 2017.

(b) Complete the following sentence. **(1 mark)**

The latest date for filing its CT600 corporation tax return is 31 March 2018.

Task 7 (8 marks)

(a) Identify whether the following statements are true or false:

(6 marks)

Statement	True ✓	False ✓
An individual who files a paper self assessment return on 25 January following the end of the tax year will incur a penalty of £100.	✓	
An individual may amend a self assessment return up to one year after the submission date, provided it was not filed late.		✓
Charlie's accountant has found an error in Charlie's 2014 self assessment return. If Charlie admits the error to HMRC, it would be considered an unprompted error.	✓	
Late payment penalties are only payable for late payment of balancing payments, not payments on account.	✓	
To avoid a penalty, a company that commenced trading on 1 September 2016 should notify HMRC it is within the scope of corporation tax by 5 April 2017.		✓
If a company submits a CT600 for the accounting year ended 31 December 2016 on 31 August 2017, HMRC must notify the company of an enquiry by 31 December 2018.		✓

Suzie has made an unprompted disclosure to the Inland Revenue. It was considered a deliberate but not concealed error and has resulted in further tax payable of £2,000.

(b) Complete the following sentence. **(2 marks)**

She will incur a minimum penalty of £ 400 and a maximum penalty of £ 1,400.

Task 8 (5 marks)

The following statements are about how trading losses of a company can be utilised.

Identify whether the following statements are true or false.

(5 marks)

Statement	True ✓	False ✓
Trading losses can be carried forward and offset against future chargeable gains.		✓
Trading losses can be carried back to be utilised in any of the previous three years.		✓
Trading losses can be offset against current year chargeable gains.	✓	
Carrying forward trading losses is the most advantageous option for cash flow.		✓
Trading losses carried forward can only be used in the next accounting period.		✓
Trading losses must first be offset against current year total profits before being carried back to a previous period.	✓	
Trading losses are offset against total profits in priority to Gift Aid donations.	✓	

Task 9 (14 marks)

In the spaces provided below prepare notes to help with the writing of a reply to Jason's email.

(a) Briefly summarise the intermediaries (IR35) legislation.

(3 marks)

This legislation prevents personal service companies (PSC) being used to disguise permanent employment. It is applied if the relationship between the worker and the client would be considered to be an employment relationship if the existence of the PSC was ignored.

When the legislation is applied, a deemed employment income tax charge is charged on the PSC.

(b) An explanation of how income is taxed differently under IR35 legislation compared to how Jason's income from the company is currently taxed. (3 marks)

Under IR35 legislation, the deemed employment income tax charge is subject to income tax and National Insurance. This is the same as for employment income but different to how most of Jason's income is currently taxed.

Currently Jason receives a small salary of £1,000pm that is taxed as employment income. However, most of his income is received as dividends which are not subject to national insurance.

Finally, only expenses typically tax deductible for employees are allowable under the IR35 legislation. However, a larger range of tax deductible expenses are available to trading companies not affected by IR35.

(c) Explain which aspects of the work suggest IR35 may apply and which suggest IR35 may NOT apply. (7 marks)

The following facts about the engagement suggest IR35 may apply to this work as they are aspects of the engagement that are associated with permanent employment:

- Jason works full-time for the engager and works under a contract, and
- Jason has to exclusively provide the services.

The following facts about the engagement suggest IR35 may NOT apply to this work as they are NOT aspects of the engagement that are associated with permanent employment:

- Jason is allowed to provide the services through a replacement consultant if he is off sick or on holiday,
- Jason provides the services from his office at home, and
- Jason uses his own company's IT equipment in providing the services, purchased for £20,000.

(d) Reply to Jason's request for information regarding other clients' tax returns. (1 mark)

Jason should be advised that an accountant has duties and responsibilities to his/her clients and this includes maintaining client confidentiality at all times. So the firm would not be able to disclose other clients' information to third parties.

Task 10 (8 marks)

Calculate the chargeable gain on the disposal of these assets. Do not use brackets or minus signs. (8 marks)

	Painting £	Bookcase £
Proceeds	62,450	31,650
Total cost	38,700	16,650
Total indexation allowance	15,983	4,428
Gain	7,767	10,572

Task 11 (10 marks)

Calculate the total chargeable gain or loss for the disposal of these shares in October 2016 and the value of the shares carried forward after the disposal. (10 marks)

Date	Transaction	No. of shares	Unindexed value, £	Indexed value, £
March 2010	Purchase	2,500	125,000	125,000
April 2011	Bonus issue	500	0	0
		3,000	125,000	125,000
November 2012	Indexation factor 0.113			14,125
	Right issue	1,500	67,500	67,500
		4,500	192,500	206,625
October 2016	Indexation factor 0.067			13,844
		4,500	192,500	220,496
	Sale	1,250	53,472	61,241
	C/fwd	3,250	139,028	159,228

Date	Transaction	No. of shares	Unindexed value, £	Indexed value, £
Chargeable gain				
Disposal proceeds	233,750			
Cost 10/10/16	(112,500)			
Pool	(61,241)			
Gain	60,009			

AAT AQ2016 SAMPLE ASSESSMENT 2
Business Tax

You are advised to attempt sample assessment 2 online from the AAT website. This will ensure you are prepared for how the assessment will be presented on the AAT's system when you attempt the real assessment. Please access the assessment using the address below:

https://www.aat.org.uk/training/study-support/search

AAT AQ2016 SAMPLE ASSESMENT 2

BPP PRACTICE ASSESSMENT 1
BUSINESS TAX

Time allowed: 2 hours

PRACTICE ASSESMENT 1

Business Tax (BSTX)
BPP practice assessment 1

In the live assessment you will have access to the Tax tables and reference material which have been reproduced at the back of this Question Bank (see page 241–259). Please use them whilst completing this practice assessment so that you are familiar with their content.

Task 1

The statement of profit or loss for George Checkers shows the following:

	£	£
Gross profit		396,550
General expenses (see notes below)	85,480	
Irrecoverable debts (see notes below)	585	
Motor expenses (see notes below)	7,880	
Wages and salaries	54,455	
Depreciation charge	21,080	
		(169,480)
Profit for the year		227,070

Notes

General expenses include:		£
Gifts to customers – Christmas cakes costing £4.50 each		1,350
Building a new wall around car park		2,200
Irrecoverable debts are made up of:		**£**
Trade debts written-off		350
Increase in general provision		400
Trade debts recovered		(165)
		585

Motor expenses are made up of:	Private usage %	Annual expense £
George	25	6,600
Salesman	20	1,280
Capital allowances computed to be:		15,000

(a) Complete the computation provided below. Fill in all unshaded boxes. Do not use minus signs or brackets to show negative numbers.

	£
Profit for the year per accounts	
Disallowed items added back	
[A] ▼	
[B] ▼	
[C] ▼	
[D] ▼	
[E] ▼	
Total to add back	
Allowed items deducted	
[F] ▼	
Adjusted trading profits	

Picklist for A to E:

Gifts to customers – cakes
New wall
Trade debts written-off
Increase in general provision
Private motor expenses – George
Private motor expenses – salesman
Depreciation charge

Picklist for F:

Trade debts recovered
Capital allowances

(b) For the following items, tick the correct treatment when computing the adjusted trading profits:

	Allowed ✓	Disallowed – add back ✓	Disallowed – deduct ✓
Purchase of raw materials			
Private use of vehicle by an employee			
Purchase of delivery van			
Interest received on business bank account			

Task 2

(a) Jude and Kelly have been in partnership for many years making up accounts to 30 September each year. They share profits 3:1 respectively.

On 1 July 2016, Liam joined the partnership. It was agreed that Liam would be paid a salary of £6,000 per year and that profits would be shared 2:2:1 for Jude, Kelly and Liam.

For the year ended 30 September 2016, the partnership trading profit was £54,000.

Show the division of profits between the partners for the year ended 30 September 2016 in the table below. Fill in all unshaded boxes and add a 0 (zero) if necessary.

	Jude £	Kelly £	Liam £
Period to: (Insert dates as: xx/xx/xxxx)			
Division of profits			
Period to: (Insert dates as: xx/xx/xxxx)			
Salary			
Division of profits			
Total profit for y/e 30/09/2015			

(b) The following accounts have been prepared for a sole trader:

	£
Y/e 30/06/2016	45,000
Y/e 30/06/2017	42,000
Period to: 30/11/17	15,000

The trade ceased on 30 November 2017 and overlap profits from commencement were £9,500.

(i) The penultimate tax year is: (insert as xxxx/xx)

(ii) The final tax year is: (insert as xxxx/xx)

(iii) The profits for the penultimate year of trade are:

£	

(iv) The profits for the final year of trade are:

£	

Task 3

Mr Wish commenced trade on 1 July 2016. He made up his first set of accounts for six months to 31 December 2016 and yearly from then on.

The following fixed asset information is available for his first 18 months of trade:

Date	**Additions**	**Cost £**
1 July 16	New plant and machinery.	130,400
15 July 16	A car with CO_2 emissions of 120g/km. Mr Wish used this car 75% of the time for business purposes.	16,000
2 Mar 17	A car with CO_2 emissions of 190g/km. This car is used 20% of the time by a salesman for private purposes.	28,000
2 July 17	A new car for Mr Wish with CO_2 emissions of 70g/km. Mr Wish used this car 75% of the time for business purposes.	17,500
Date	**Disposals**	**Proceeds £**
15 Dec 16	Plant purchased for £32,000.	18,000
1 July 17	Mr Wish's car bought on 15 July 16.	15,300

Calculate the capital allowances for Mr Wish for the six month period ended 31 December 2016 and the year ended 31 December 2017. Show the balances to carry forward to the next accounting period.

	£	£	£	£	£	£	£

Task 4

Spire Ltd's adjusted trading profits, after deducting capital allowances was £865,000.

The company sold a piece of investment land in August 2016 realising a gain of £73,500.

Spire Ltd has one related 51% group company.

Dividends of £108,000 (net) were received from a non-related 51% group company on 31 December 2016.

Complete the following extract from the tax return for Spire Ltd for the year ended 31 December 2016 using the information below.

Tax calculation

Turnover

145	Total turnover from trade	£ . 00
150	Banks, building societies, insurance companies and other financial concerns - *put an 'X' in this box if you do not have a recognised turnover and have not made an entry in box 145*	☐

Income

155	Trading profits	£ . 00
160	Trading losses brought forward claimed against profits	£ . 00
165	Net trading profits - *box 155 minus box 160*	£ . 00
170	Bank, building society or other interest, and profits from non-trading loan relationships	£ . 00
172	Put an 'X' in box 172 if the figure in box 170 is net of carrying back a deficit from a later accounting period	☐
175	Annual payments not otherwise charged to Corporation Tax and from which Income Tax has not been deducted	£ . 00

CT600(2016) Version 3 Page 2 HMRC 04/15

Income *continued*

180	Non-exempt dividends or distributions from non-UK resident companies	£ . 0 0
185	Income from which Income Tax has been deducted	£ . 0 0
190	Income from a property business	£ . 0 0
195	Non-trading gains on intangible fixed assets	£ . 0 0
200	Tonnage Tax profits	£ . 0 0
205	Income not falling under any other heading	£ . 0 0

Chargeable gains

210	Gross chargeable gains	£ . 0 0
215	Allowable losses including losses brought forward	£ . 0 0
220	Net chargeable gains - *box 210 minus box 215*	£ . 0 0

Profits before deductions and reliefs

225	Losses brought forward against certain investment income	£ . 0 0
230	Non-trade deficits on loan relationships (including interest) and derivative contracts (financial instruments) brought forward	£ . 0 0
235	Profits before other deductions and reliefs - *net sum of boxes 165 to 205 and 220 minus sum of boxes 225 and 230*	£ . 0 0

CT600(2016) Version 3 Page 3 HMRC 04/15

(Adapted from HMRC, 2016)

Task 5

(a) A company made up accounts to 31 December 2015. It decides to make up its next set of accounts to 31 March 2017.

Identify how the company will deal with its capital allowances in the long period of account. Tick ONE box.

	✓
One computation from 1 January 2016 to 31 March 2017	
Two computations: one from 1 January 2016 to 31 March 2016 and one from 1 April 2016 to 31 March 2017	
Two computations: one from 1 January 2016 to 31 December 2016 and one from 1 January 2017 to 31 March 2017	
It can deal with the computation for whatever period the company chooses	

(b) Abbey Ltd has the following information for the year ended 31 March 2017.

The adjusted trading profit, after deducting capital allowances of £37,430, was £620,843.

The company sold a piece of investment land in December 2016 realising a gain of £67,817.

Abbey Ltd has one wholly owned subsidiary.

(i) Abbey Ltd's taxable total profits are:

£	

(ii) The corporation tax payable for the year ended 31 March 2017 is:

£	

(iii) The due date for payment is: (insert as xx/xx/xxxx)

(c) T Ltd, a large company, has a corporation tax liability of £600,000 in respect of its accounting year ended 31 December 2016.

Identify the date the company will be required to pay its FINAL instalment of the liability. Tick ONE box.

	✓
14 October 2016	
14 January 2017	
14 April 2017	
1 October 2017	

Task 6

Mina is a client of yours. She has tax payable for 2016/17 of £4,225, but was not required to make any payments on account for this tax year.

Mina is looking for advice about when she needs to pay this tax. She has also advised you that she accidentally forgot to include quite a substantial trading invoice in her tax return for 2015/16, and is wondering what to do about this and whether she might incur a penalty.

In the box below respond to Mina's query by explaining:

(a) **When she should pay the 2016/17 tax liability**

(b) **How much each payment on account will be for 2017/18 and when these should be paid**

(c) **When the balancing payment 2017/18 would be due and how this is calculated**

(d) **The penalty that she may incur for a careless (non deliberate) error on her return, and what she could do to try and reduce this penalty**

Task 7

Crystal is a sole trader who has been trading for many years, has taxable trading profits of £91,750 for the year ended 31 December 2016.

Crystal's Class 2 NIC liability for 2016/17 is: (show your answer to the nearest penny)

£		.	

Crystal's Class 4 NIC liability for 2016/17 is: (show your answer to the nearest penny)

£		.	

Pearl is a sole trader who has been trading for many years. She has taxable trading profits of £27,300 for the year ended 31 December 2016.

Pearl's Class 2 NIC liability for 2016/17 is: (show your answer to the nearest penny)

£		.	

Pearl's Class 4 NIC liability for 2016/17 is: (show your answer to the nearest penny)

£		.	

Task 8

(a) Identify whether the following statements are true or false.

	True ✓	False ✓
A sole trader must make a claim to set a loss made in 2016/17 against total income in 2016/17 before making a claim to set the loss against total income in 2015/16		
A sole trader can carry trade losses forward and choose the best year to use them		
A sole trader can only offset trading losses brought forward against profits of the same trade		

(b) A limited company makes a trading loss of £47,300 in its year ended 31 March 2017. It has also made a chargeable gain of £52,350 in the same period, and has capital losses brought forward of £5,200. The company has a policy of claiming relief for its losses as soon as possible.

(i) **The amount of trading loss that can be claimed against profits in year ended 31 March 2017 is:**

£	

(ii) **The amount of trading loss that can be carried forward to the year ended 31 March 2018 is:**

£	

Task 9

A small or medium sized company incurring qualifying Research and Development costs can obtain extra relief for those costs.

(a) Briefly define a small or medium sized company, state what those qualifying costs may comprise, and how the extra relief is calculated.

The generous relief for R&D expenditure may lead to tax losses.

(b) Briefly explain the extra option a company has if the tax loss is created by R&D relief.

Task 10

(a) For the following disposals, tick if it would be exempt or chargeable:

	Exempt ✓	Chargeable ✓
Disposal of a vintage car worth £40,000		
Gift of land to a charity		
Gift of jewellery on the taxpayer's death		

(b) Nick bought a five-acre plot of land for £50,000. He sold three acres of the land at auction for £105,000. He had spent £2,500 installing drainage on the three acres which he sold. His disposal costs were £1,500. The market value of the remaining two acres at the date of sale was £45,000.

Calculate the chargeable gain on the disposal of the three acres of land using the table below (do not use brackets or minus signs).

	£
Gross proceeds	
Costs of disposal	
Net proceeds	
Cost	
Enhancement expenditure	
Chargeable gain	

Task 11

In May 2016, Green Ltd sold 4,000 of the shares it held in Blue Ltd for £130,000. These shares had been acquired as follows:

	No. of shares	£
April 1989	2,000	25,000
June 1994	2,000	35,000
July 1997 – bonus issue	1 for 10	
September 2002 – rights issue	1 for 5	£10 per share

Indexation factors:

April 1989 to June 1994	0.266
June 1994 to July 1997	0.088
June 1994 to September 2002	0.227
July 1997 to September 2002	0.128
September 2002 to May 2016	0.468

Calculate the chargeable gain on the sale of these shares in May 2016.

BPP PRACTICE ASSESSMENT 1 BUSINESS TAX

ANSWERS

Business Tax (BSTX)
BPP practice assessment 1

Task 1

(a)

	£
Profit for the year per accounts	227,070
Disallowed items added back	
Gifts to customers – cakes	1,350
New wall	2,200
Increase in general provision	400
Private motor expenses – George	1,650
Depreciation charge	21,080
Total to add back	26,680
Allowed items deducted	
Capital allowances	15,000
Adjusted trading profits	238,750

(b)

	Allowed ✓	Disallowed – add back ✓	Disallowed – deduct ✓
Purchase of raw materials	✓		
Private use of vehicle by an employee	✓		
Purchase of delivery van		✓	
Interest received on business bank account			✓

Task 2

(a)

	Jude £	Kelly £	Liam £
Period to:			
30/06/2016			
Division of profits (3:1)	30,375	10,125	0
Period to:			
30/09/2016			
Salary (3 months)	0	0	1,500
Division of profits (2:2:1)	4,800	4,800	2,400
Total profit for y/e 30/09/2016	35,175	14,925	3,900

(b)

(i) The penultimate tax year is:

2016/17

(ii) The final tax year is:

2017/18

(iii) The profits for the penultimate year of trade are:

£ 45,000

(iv) The profits for the final year of trade are:

£ 47,500

Working:

(£42,000 + £15,000 – £9,500)

Task 3

	AIA £	Main pool £	Special rate pool £	Owner's car £		Allowances £
Period to 31 December 16						
Additions:						
Plant and machinery	130,400					
Car				16,000		
AIA £200,000 × 6/12	(100,000)					100,000
	30,400	30,400				
Disposal		(18,000)				
		12,400				
WDA @ 18% × 6/12				(1,440)	× 75%	1,080
WDA @ 18% × 6/12		(1,116)				1,116
Capital allowances						102,196
Year end 31 December 17		11,284		14,560		
Disposal				(15,300)		
Balancing charge				(740)	× 75%	(555)
Additions:						
Car – salesman			28,000			
Car – Mr Wish				17,500		
WDA @ 8 %			(2,240)			2,240
FYA @ 100%				(17,500)	× 75%	13,125
WDA @ 18%		(2,031)				2,031
Capital allowances						16,841
c/f		9,253	25,760	0		

Task 4

Box 155 £865,000
Box 165 £865,000
Box 210 £73,500
Box 220 £73,500
Box 235 £938,500

Note. Dividends from a non-related 51% group company are not taxable.

Task 5

(a)

	✓
One computation from 1 January 2016 to 31 March 2017	
Two computations: one from 1 January 2016 to 31 March 2016 and one from 1 April 2016 to 31 March 2017	
Two computations: one from 1 January 2016 to 31 December 2016 and one from 1 January 2017 to 31 March 2017	✓
It can deal with the computation for whatever period the company chooses	

(b) **(i)** Abbey Ltd's taxable total profits are:

£	688,660

Working:

(£620,843 + £67,817)

(ii) The corporation tax payable for the year ended 31 March 2017 is:

£	137,732

Working:

	£
£688,660 × 20%	137,732

(iii) The due date for payment is:

01/01/2018

Abbey Ltd is not a large company so pays its corporation tax 9 months and one day after the end of the accounting period.

(c)

	✓
14 October 2016	
14 January 2017	
14 April 2017	✓
1 October 2017	

Task 6

(a) The date by which the tax liability for 2016/17 should be paid is 31 January 2018.

(b) There will be two payments on account for 2017/18. Each will be calculated as 50% of the tax liability for the previous tax year (2016/17). The amount will therefore be £2,112.50 (£4,225 ÷ 2), and will be payable on 31 January during the tax year (31 January 2018) and 31 July after the end of the tax year (31 July 2018).

(c) A balancing payment will be due on 31 January after the end of the tax year (31 January 2019) which will be calculated as the actual amount payable for 2017/18 less the two payments on account.

(d) A penalty may be imposed on Mina as she has been careless and not taken reasonable care when filing her return. The penalty will be 30% of the potential lost revenue (PLR) to HMRC as a result of the error. This may be reduced to 0% if Mina makes an unprompted disclosure of the error, which would be before Mina has reason to believe HMRC might discover the error. Otherwise the penalty could be reduced to 15% of PLR and classed as a prompted disclosure.

Task 7

Crystal's Class 2 NIC liability for 2016/17 is: (show your answer to the nearest penny)

£	145	.	60

Working:

(£2.80 × 52)

Crystal's Class 4 NIC liability for 2016/17 is: (show your answer to the nearest penny)

£	4,119	.	60

Working:

£(43,000 – 8,060) × 9% + £(91,750 – 43,000) × 2%

= (3,144.60) + (975.00)

Pearl's Class 2 NIC liability for 2016/17 is: (show your answer to the nearest penny)

£	145	.	60

Working:

(£2.80 × 52)

Pearl's Class 4 NIC liability for 2016/17 is: (show your answer to the nearest penny)

£	1,731	.	60

Working:

£(27,300 – 8,060) × 9%

Task 8

(a)

	True ✓	False ✓
A sole trader must make a claim to set a loss made in 2016/17 against total income in 2016/17 before making a claim to set the loss against total income in 2015/16		✓
A sole trader can carry trade losses forward and choose the best year to use them.		✓
A sole trader can only offset trading losses brought forward against profits of the same trade.	✓	

A sole trader can make a claim to deduct the loss from total income in the tax year preceding the tax year in which the loss is made whether or not he makes a claim to set it against total income in the tax year of the loss.

A sole trader must offset losses carried forward against the first available profits of the same trade.

(b) **(i)** The amount of trading loss that can be claimed against profits in year ended 31 March 2017 is:

£	47,150

Working:

(£52,350 - £5,200)

(ii) The amount of trading loss that can be carried forward to the year ended 31 March 2018 is:

£	150

Task 9

(a)

To be classed as small or medium sized the company must have fewer than 500 employees and have either Turnover of less than 100 million Euros or a Balance Sheet of less than 86 million Euros.

Qualifying research and development costs would include items such as R&D staff costs, consumables, software and utilities.

The relief is 230% of the qualifying revenue expenses.

(b)

The company may surrender its loss in return for an R&D tax credit.

This is calculated as 14.5% of the surrenderable loss, capped at the company's PAYE bill.

Task 10

(a)

	Exempt ✓	Chargeable ✓
Disposal of a vintage car worth £40,000	✓	
Gift of land to a charity	✓	
Gift of jewellery on the taxpayer's death	✓	

(b)

	£
Gross proceeds	105,000
Costs of disposal	1,500
Net proceeds	103,500
Cost (w)	35,000
Enhancement expenditure	2,500
Chargeable gain	66,000

Working: cost = $\frac{105,000}{105,000 + 45,000} \times £50,000$ (35,000)

Task 11

	No. of shares	Cost £	Indexed cost £
FA 1985 pool			
April 1989	2,000	25,000	25,000
Index to June 1994 0.266 × £25,000			6,650
Addition	2,000	35,000	35,000
	4,000	60,000	66,650
Bonus issue (N)	400	–	–
	4,400	60,000	66,650
Index to September 2002 0.227 × £66,650			15,130
	4,400	60,000	81,780
Rights issue	880	8,800	8,800
	5,280	68,800	90,580
Index to May 2016 0.468 × £90,580			42,391
	5,280	68,800	132,971
Less sale	(4,000)	(52,121)	(100,736)
	1,280	16,679	32,235
Gain			£
Disposal proceeds			130,000
Less cost			(52,121)
Less indexation £(100,736 – 52,121)			(48,615)
Chargeable gain			29,264

Note. There is no need to compute indexation to the date of the bonus issue.

BPP PRACTICE ASSESSMENT 2
BUSINESS TAX

Time allowed: 2 hours

Business Tax (BSTX)
BPP practice assessment 2

In the live assessment you will have access to the Tax tables and reference material which have been reproduced at the back of this Question Bank (see page 241–259). Please use them whilst completing this practice assessment so that you are familiar with their content.

Task 1

The statement of profit or loss for Henry Ltd for the year to 31 December 2016 shows the following information:

	£	£
Gross profit		487,500
Profit on sale of shares		12,850
Dividends received		4,500
Property business income		7,500
		512,350
General expenses (note 1)	240,780	
Wages and salaries	120,650	
Administrative expenses	87,230	
Depreciation charge	14,600	
		(463,260)
Profit for the year		49,090

Notes

1 **General expenses**

These include:

	£
Qualifying charitable donation (paid July 2016)	3,500
Entertaining customers	8,450

2 Capital allowances

The capital allowances for the year ended 31 December 2016 are £8,750.

(a) Complete the computation. Do not use minus signs or brackets to show negative figures. Please keep your selected answers in the same order as they appear in the picklist.

Profit	49,090
Add back (Picklist 1)	
▼	
▼	
▼	
Total added back	
Deduct (Picklist 2)	
▼	
▼	
▼	
▼	
Adjusted trading profits	

Picklist 1:

Qualifying charitable donation (paid July 2016)
Entertaining customers
Wages and salaries
Administrative expenses
Depreciation charge

Picklist 2:

Profit on sale of shares
Dividends received
Property business income
Administrative expenses
Depreciation charge
Capital allowances

(b) For each of the following items, pick the correct treatment in relation to the computation of the taxable profit.

Capital allowances	▼
Staff party £10 per head	▼
Purchase of new motor vehicle	▼

Picklist:

Allowed
Disallowed and add back
Disallowed and deduct

Task 2

Mustafa has been trading for many years, making up accounts to 31 March.

His capital allowances balances brought forward at 1 April 2016 were as follows:

Main pool	£13,291
Car for Mustafa, 30% private usage	£8,745

The following capital transactions were made in the period:

		£
Additions		
10.04.16	Plant and machinery	58,100
15.04.16	Car for Mustafa, CO_2 emissions 70 g/km, 40% private usage	24,500
22.06.16	Plant and machinery	183,750
Disposal		
15.04.16	Mustafa's previous car	8,000
3.05.16	Plant and machinery (original cost £4,100)	5,970

Using the proforma layout provided, calculate the capital allowances for the year ended 31 March 2017.

	AIA £	Main pool £	Private use car (70%) £	Private use car (60%) £	Allowan[ces] £

Task 3

(a) Sayed started trading on 1 January 2016. He makes up his accounts to 30 April each year. The profits were calculated as:

	£
Period to 30 April 2016	20,000
Year to 30 April 2017	36,000
Year to 30 April 2018	42,000

Calculate the taxable profits and state the tax year and basis period for the first three tax years of trading. Insert the tax year dates as XXXX/XX (eg 2015/16) and the basis period dates as XX/XX/XXXX (eg 01/12/2015).

	Tax year XXXX/XX	Basis period XX/XX/XXXX – XX/XX/XXXX	Profit £
First year	/	–	
Second year	/	–	
Third year	/	–	

His overlap profits are:

£	

(b) Peter has been in business for several years with a year end of 30 September. In 2017 he decided to change his accounting date to 31 March. His overlap profit on commencement was £3,000 for six months and his recent profits were:

	£
Year ended 30 September 2015	12,000
Year to 30 September 2016	18,000
Period ended 31 March 2017	6,000
Year ended 31 March 2018	24,000

Calculate the taxable profits and state the tax year and basis period for the year of change and the years before and after. Insert the tax year dates as XXXX/XX (eg 2016/17) and the basis period dates as XX/XX/XXXX (eg 30/09/2016).

Tax year XXXX/XX	Basis period XX/XX/XXXX – XX/XX/XXXX	Profit £
/	–	
/	–	
/	–	

Task 4

Aggie Tring has carried on business for many years as a furniture restorer making up accounts to 31 December each year.

The following information is relevant to her period of account to 31 December 2016:

	£
Revenue	144,000
Cost of materials used in restoration	20,000
Travel (20% private)	5,700
Electricity	900
Insurance	360
Office costs	1,800
Bank charges	200
Accountancy	550
Machinery purchased	5,000

Using this information, complete the self employment page.

Business expenses

Please read the *Self-employment (full) notes* before filling in this section.

Total expenses	Disallowable expenses
If your annual turnover was below £83,000 you may just put your total expenses in box 31	Use this column if the figures in boxes 17 to 30 include disallowable amounts
17 Cost of goods bought for resale or goods used £ .00	32 £ .00
18 Construction industry – *payments to subcontractors* £ .00	33 £ .00
19 Wages, salaries and other staff costs £ .00	34 £ .00
20 Car, van and travel expenses £ .00	35 £ .00
21 Rent, rates, power and insurance costs £ .00	36 £ .00
22 Repairs and renewals of property and equipment £ .00	37 £ .00
23 Phone, fax, stationery and other office costs £ .00	38 £ .00
24 Advertising and business entertainment costs £ .00	39 £ .00
25 Interest on bank and other loans £ .00	40 £ .00
26 Bank, credit card and other financial charges £ .00	41 £ .00
27 Irrecoverable debts written off £ .00	42 £ .00
28 Accountancy, legal and other professional fees £ .00	43 £ .00
29 Depreciation and loss/profit on sale of assets £ .00	44 £ .00
30 Other business expenses £ .00	45 £ .00
31 Total expenses (total of boxes 17 to 30) £ .00	46 Total disallowable expenses (total of boxes 32 to 45) £ .00

SA103F 2015 Page SEF 2

(Adapted from HMRC, 2016)

Task 5

A company made up accounts to 31 March 2016. It decides to make up its next set of accounts to 30 September 2017.

(a) Show how each of the following would be allocated for the long period of account.

	Amount accrued in period ✓	Time apportioned ✓	Period in which it arose ✓
Trading profits			
Business property income			
Qualifying charitable donation			
Chargeable gains			
Non trading interest received			

(b) Tick the correct box to show whether the following statements are true or false:

	True ✓	False ✓
A company can offset its allowable losses on the disposal of chargeable assets against trading profits.		
A company can carry back its trading losses to set against total profits of the previous 12 months before offsetting losses against current year total profits.		
The carry forward of a company's trading loss to offset against the first available profits of the same trade is automatic and compulsory.		

A company has the following information for the year ended 31 December 2016:

- Taxable total profits are £495,000.
- Dividends received (net) are £10,800.
- The company has two related 51% group companies.

(c) What is the first date by which the company has to pay some or all of its corporation tax liability? (XX/XX/XXXX)

Task 6

Polly is a sole trader who has taxable trading profits of £63,000 in 2016/17.

The amount chargeable to national insurance Class 4 contributions at 9% is:

£	

The amount chargeable to national insurance Class 4 contributions at 2% is:

£	

The total amount of national insurance payable by Polly in 2016/17 is:

£		.	

Task 7

(a) (i) The maximum penalty for failure to keep records for each tax year or accounting period is:

	✓
£4,000	
£3,000	
£2,500	
£1,500	

(ii) The maximum penalty for a deliberate but not concealed failure to notify chargeability as a percentage of Potential Lost Revenue is:

	✓
70%	
35%	
20%	
15%	

(iii) A taxpayer files his tax return for 2016/17 online on 15 March 2018. His tax liability for the year is £2,000.

The maximum penalty for late filing is:

	✓
£2,000	
£300	
£200	
£100	

(b) Holly has a liability to capital gains tax in 2016/17.

(i) She must pay the capital gains tax due by: (insert dates as xx/xx/xxxx)

Holly is also required to make payments on account for her 2016/17 income tax liability.

(ii) She must make payments on account for 2016/17 by:

and

(iii) She must pay the balancing payment by:

Task 8

JDP, a sole trader who has been trading for many years, made a trading profit of £4,500 in his year ended 31 January 2016, a trading loss of £45,000 in his year ended 31 January 2017, and he predicts trading profits to be £5,000 for year ended 31 January 2018. Each tax year he also receives rental income of £9,000, and in December 2016 he sold a painting and made a chargeable gain of £17,000.

JDP has a policy of claiming the maximum amount of loss relief as early as possible, in all possible ways.

How much trading loss will JDP relieve against net income in 2015/16?

£	

How much trading loss will JDP relieve against net income in 2016/17?

£	

How much trading loss will JDP relieve against his chargeable gain in 2016/17?

£	

Tick the correct box to show whether the following statement is true or false:

	True ✓	False ✓
In 2016/17 JDP could choose to just set the loss against the capital gain, so as not to lose the benefit of his personal allowance		

What is the maximum trading loss JDP can relieve in 2017/18?

£	

Task 9

(a) Fill in the blanks using the picklist below:

An employed person usually has a contract ____________ service, where as a self-employed person will have a contract ____________ services.

Picklist:

for
of

(b) Fred is doing some work for Howard Limited. Tick the relevant column to show whether the following factors would tend to imply that Fred is employed or self-employed:

	Employed ✓	Self-employed ✓
Fred has permission to work for several clients		
Howard Ltd pay Fred sick and holiday pay		
Howard Ltd provide all the equipment which Fred needs		
Fred has control over when and where he performs the work		

Task 10

Purple Ltd had the following transactions in the shares of Yellow Ltd:

May 1989	Purchased 4,000 shares for £8,000
May 2003	Took up one for two rights issue at £3 per share
October 2016	Sold all the shares for £32,000

Assumed Indexation factors

May 1989 to May 2003	0.578
May 2003 to October 2016	0.448

Using the proforma layout provided, calculate the chargeable gain arising from the sale of the shares in Yellow Ltd.

Share pool

	No. of shares	Cost £	Indexed cost £

Gain

	£

Task 11

Georgia sold her business which she had run for twenty years to Milly on 10 October 2016. The only chargeable asset was her shop which Georgia had bought in February 2009 for £82,500. She spent £17,000 on building an extension in June 2011. The sale proceeds relating to the shop were £225,000. Georgia claimed entrepreneurs' relief on the disposal.

(a) Using the proforma layout provided, calculate Georgia's capital gains tax liability for 2016/17. She had made no other chargeable gains during the year.

	£
Sale proceeds	
Cost	
Enhancement expenditure	
Net gain	
Annual exempt amount	
Taxable gain	
CGT payable	

On 1 November 2016 Mike sold a factory used in his business for £600,000. The factory had cost £175,000. Mike had purchased a replacement factory for £750,000 on 1 September 2016.

(b) How much of Mike's capital gain on the disposal of the original factory can be deferred by a rollover relief claim?

	✓
£150,000	
£575,000	
£175,000	
£425,000	

(c) If Mike's replacement factory had instead cost him £500,000, the amount of the gain that would be chargeable to CGT in 2016/17 is:

£	

BPP PRACTICE ASSESSMENT 2
BUSINESS TAX

ANSWERS

Business Tax (BSTX)
BPP practice assessment 2

Task 1

(a)

Profit	49,090
Add back	
Qualifying charitable donation (paid July 2016)	3,500
Entertaining customers	8,450
Depreciation charge	14,600
Total added back	26,550
Deduct	
Profit on sale of shares	12,850
Dividends received	4,500
Property business income	7,500
Capital allowances	8,750
Adjusted trading profits	42,040

(b)

Capital allowances	Allowed
Staff party £10 per head	Allowed
Purchase of new motor vehicle	Disallowed and add back

Task 2

Year ended 31 March 2017

	AIA £	Main pool £	Private use car (70%) £	Private use car (60%) £	Allowances £
b/f		13,291	8,745		
AIA additions					
April 2016	58,100				
June 2016	183,750				
Car April 2016				24,500	
AIA	(200,000)				200,000
Transfer to pool		41,850			
Disposals		(4,100)	(8,000)		
		51,041			
BA			745 × 70%		522
WDA @ 18%		(9,187)			9,187
FYA @ 100%				(24,500) × 60%	14,700
c/f		41,854		0	
Total allowances					224,409

Task 3

(a)

	Tax year XXXX/XX	Basis period XX/XX/XXXX – XX/XX/XXXX	Profit £
First year	2015/16	01/01/2016 – 05/04/2016	15,000
Second year	2016/17	01/01/2016 – 31/12/2016	44,000
Third year	2017/18	01/05/2016 – 30/04/2017	36,000

Working:

Second year: Period ending 30 April 2016 plus 8 months to 31 December 2016

£20,000 + (8/12 × £36,000) = £44,000

His overlap profits are:

£	39,000

Working:

Overlap period: 1 January 2016 to 5 April 2016 and 1 May 2016 to 31 December 2016

Overlap profits: ¾ × £20,000 + 8/12 × £36,000

(b)

Tax year XXXX/XX	Basis period XX/XX/XXXX – XX/XX/XXXX	Profit £
2015/16	01/10/2014 – 30/09/2015	12,000
2016/17	01/10/2015 – 31/03/2017	21,000
2017/18	01/04/2017 – 31/03/2018	24,000

Working:

The year of change is 2016/17.

For 2015/16 and 2017/18 the profits are allocated on a current year basis.

For 2016/17 there are two periods ending in the tax year. In this case, we tax them both and relieve overlap:

Year ended 30 September 2016 (12 months)	18,000
Period ended 31 March 2017 (6 months)	6,000
Relieve overlap to bring profits down to 12 months	(3,000)
Taxable profits 2016/17	21,000

Task 4

Box 17	£20,000
Box 20	£5,700
Box 21	£1,260
Box 23	£1,800
Box 26	£200
Box 28	£550
Box 31	£29,510
Box 35	£1,140
Box 46	£1,140

Task 5

(a)

	Amount accrued in period ✓	Time apportioned ✓	Period in which it arose ✓
Trading profits		✓	
Business property income		✓	
Qualifying charitable donation			✓
Chargeable gains			✓
Non trading interest received	✓		

(b)

	True ✓	False ✓
A company can offset its allowable losses on the disposal of chargeable assets against trading profits.		✓
A company can carry back its trading losses to set against total profits of the previous 12 months before offsetting losses against current year total profits.		✓
The carry forward of a company's trading loss to offset against the first available profits of the same trade is automatic and compulsory.	✓	

A company can offset its allowable losses on the disposal of chargeable assets only against chargeable gains.

A company must offset trading losses in the current period first, whereas an individual trader can offset trading losses in the current and prior year in any order.

(c)

14/07/2016

Working:

Annual profit limit = £1,500,000/3 = £500,000 (share with 2 other related companies)

Augmented profits = £495,000 + (£10,800 x 100/90) = £507,000

Hence the company is large for corporation tax payment purposes.

Task 6

The amount chargeable to national insurance Class 4 contributions at 9% is:

£	34,940

Working:

£(43,000 – 8,060)

The amount chargeable to national insurance Class 4 contributions at 2% is:

£	20,000

Working:

£(63,000 – 43,000)

The total amount of national insurance payable by Polly for 2016/17 is:

£	3,690	.	20

Working:

Class 2 = £2.80 × 52 weeks = £145.60
Class 4 = £34,940 × 9% + £20,000 × 2% = £3,544.60

Task 7

(a) **(i)**

	✓
£4,000	
£3,000	✓
£2,500	
£1,500	

(ii)

	✓
70%	✓
35%	
20%	
15%	

(iii)

	✓
£2,000	
£300	
£200	
£100	✓

Initial penalty for filing return late is £100. As it is less than 3 months late no further penalty is payable.

(b) **(i)** She must pay the capital gains tax due by:

31/01/2018

(ii) She must make payments on account for 2016/17 by:

31/01/2017

and

31/07/2017

(iii) She must pay the balancing payment by:

31/01/2018

Task 8

The trading loss which JDP will relieve against net income in 15/16 is:

£	13,500

(£4,500 + £9,000) The loss cannot be restricted to save the personal allowance

The trading loss which JDP will relieve against net income in 2016/17 is:

£	9,000

The loss cannot be restricted to save the personal allowance

The amount of trading loss which JDP will relieve against his chargeable gain of 2016/17 is:

£	17,000

The loss cannot be restricted to save the annual exempt amount (only capital losses brought forward can be restricted in this way).

	True ✓	False ✓
In 2016/17 JDP could choose to just set the loss against the capital gain, so as not to lose the benefit of his personal allowance		✓

In order to use the trading loss against the gain, JDP must offset the loss against net income first, despite the fact that it would have been covered by his personal allowance.

The maximum trading loss JDP can relieve in 2017/18 is:

£	5,000

Losses can only be offset against trading profits when carried forward.

Task 9

(a) An employed person usually has a contract [of] service, whereas a self-employed person will have a contract [for] services.

(b)

	Employed ✓	Self-employed ✓
Fred has permission to work for several clients		✓
Howard Ltd pay Fred sick and holiday pay	✓	
Howard Ltd provide all the equipment which Fred needs	✓	
Fred has control over when and where he performs the work		✓

Task 10

Share pool

	No. of shares	Cost £	Indexed cost £
May 1989	4,000	8,000	8,000
Indexed rise to May 2003			
£8,000 × 0.578			4,624
			12,624
Rights issue 1:2 @ £3	2,000	6,000	6,000
	6,000	14,000	18,624
Indexed rise to October 2016			
£18,624 × 0.448			8,344
	6,000	14,000	26,968

Gain

	£
Disposal proceeds	32,000
Less cost	(14,000)
	18,000
Less indexation (£26,968 – £14,000)	(12,968)
Chargeable gain	5,032

Task 11

(a)

	£
Sale proceeds	225,000
Cost	(82,500)
Enhancement expenditure	(17,000)
Net gain	125,500
Annual exempt amount	(11,100)
Taxable gain	114,400
CGT payable @ 10%	11,440

(b)

	✓
£150,000	
£575,000	
£175,000	
£425,000	✓

Working:

	£
Proceeds	600,000
Less cost	(175,000)
Chargeable gain	425,000

Mike reinvested all of the proceeds in a replacement business asset in the period 12 months before/3 years after the disposal so the whole gain of £425,000 can be rolled-over.

(c)

£	100,000

This is the amount of proceeds that have not been reinvested.

BPP PRACTICE ASSESSMENT 3
BUSINESS TAX

Time allowed: 2 hours

PRACTICE ASSESSMENT 3

Business Tax (BSTX)
BPP practice assessment 3

In the live assessment you will have access to the Tax tables and reference material which have been reproduced at the back of this Question Bank (see page 241–259). Please use them whilst completing this practice assessment so that you are familiar with their content.

Task 1

You have been given the following information about Robbie Ltd that relates to the year ended 31 March 2017:

	£	£
Gross profit		801,220
Profit on sale of shares		45,777
Dividends received		40,500
		887,497
General expenses (note 1)	455,100	
Administrative expenses	122,010	
Wages and salaries	137,567	(714,677)
Profit for the year		172,820

Note.

1 General expenses:

These include:

	£
Qualifying charitable donation	5,000
Parking fines paid for a director	160
Depreciation charge	65,230
Subscription to a trade association	1,000
Donation to a political party	850

Note.

2 Capital allowances:

These have already been calculated at £38,750.

(a) Complete the computation. Do not use minus signs or brackets to show negative figures. Please keep your selected answers in the same order as they appear in the picklist.

Profit	172,820
Disallowed items added back (Picklist 1)	
▼	
▼	
▼	
▼	
Total added back	
Allowed items deducted (Picklist 2)	
▼	
▼	
▼	
Total deducted	
Adjusted trading profits	

Picklist 1:

Qualifying charitable donation
Parking fines paid for a director
Depreciation charge
Subscription to a trade association
Donation to a political party
Administrative expenses
Wages and salaries

Picklist 2:

Profit on sale of shares
Dividends received
Administrative expenses
Wages and salaries
Capital allowances

(b) Identify whether the following statements are true or false.

	True ✓	False ✓
Badges of trade have developed mainly through case law.		
If a trader inherits an asset and he sells it shortly afterwards, it will appear likely that he is trading.		
If a trader enhances an asset to make it more desirable to a buyer, this is indicative of trading.		

Task 2

Gerry and Harold have been in partnership for many years making up accounts to 31 December each year sharing profits 2:1 respectively.

On 1 January 2017, Iris joined the partnership. Profits are then shared 2:2:1 for Gerry, Harold and Iris.

For the year ended 31 December 2016, the partnership trading profit was £27,000 and for the year ended 31 December 2017 was £35,000.

(a) Using the proforma layout provided, show the division of profit between the partners for the year ended 31 December 2016 and 31 December 2017. Fill in all boxes and add a 0 (zero) if necessary.

	Total £	Gerry £	Harold £	Iris £
Year ended 31.12.16				
Year ended 31.12.17				

(b) The taxable trading profit for each partner for 2016/17 is:

Gerry:

£	

Harold:

£	

Iris:

£	

Task 3

Ian Goodwin commenced trading on 1 January 2017, and made his first accounts up to 31 March 2018. Ian Goodwin's capital transactions from the date of commencement are:

Additions:		**£**
1 May 2017	Plant and machinery	239,750
1 May 2017	Motor van	35,500
1 October 2017	Plant and machinery	8,500
1 November 2017	Car, 30% private usage by Ian (CO_2 emissions 172g/km)	9,600
15 January 2018	Car, 20% private usage by an employee (CO_2 emissions 72g/km)	12,500

Calculate the capital allowances for the 15-month period ended 31 March 2018. Assume that the rates and allowances remain unchanged going forward.

Task 4

You act for Freshly Fish, a partnership of fishmongers. The partners are Fred Fisher and his son George. The partnership profits are divided 2:1 between Fred and George. The partnership makes up accounts to 31 March each year.

The following information relates to the year to 31 March 2017:

	£
Revenue	210,000
Cost of fish sold	70,000
Allowable expenses	69,710
Capital allowances	13,200

Use this information to complete page 6 of the partnership tax return for Fred Fisher.

PARTNERSHIP STATEMENT (SHORT) for the year ended 5 April 2017

Please read these instructions before completing the Statement

Use these pages to allocate partnership income if the only income for the relevant return period was trading and professional income or taxed interest and alternative finance receipts from banks and building societies. Otherwise you must download or ask the SA Orderline for the 'Partnership Statement (Full)' pages to record details of the allocation of all the partnership income. Go to **www.gov.uk/self-assessment-forms-and-helpsheets**

Step 1 Fill in boxes 1 to 29 and boxes A and B as appropriate. Get the figures you need from the relevant boxes in the Partnership Tax Return. Complete a separate Statement for each accounting period covered by this Partnership Tax Return and for each trade or profession carried on by the partnership.

Step 2 Then allocate the amounts in boxes 11 to 29 attributable to each partner using the allocation columns on this page and page 7, read the Partnership Tax Return Guide, go to **www.gov.uk/self-assessment-forms-and-helpsheets**
If the partnership has more than 3 partners, please photocopy page 7.

Step 3 Each partner will need a copy of their allocation of income to fill in their personal tax return.

PARTNERSHIP INFORMATION

If the partnership business includes a trade or profession, enter here the accounting period for which appropriate items in this statement are returned.

Start **1** / /

End **2** / /

Nature of trade **3**

MIXED PARTNERSHIPS

Tick here if this Statement is drawn up using Corporation Tax rules **4**

Tick here if this Statement is drawn up using tax rules for non-residents **5**

Individual partner details

6 Name of partner

Address

Postcode

Date appointed as a partner (if during 2014–15 or 2015–16) **7** / /

Partner's Unique Taxpayer Reference (UTR) **8**

Date ceased to be a partner (if during 2014–15 or 2015–16) **9** / /

Partner's National Insurance number **10**

Partnership's profits, losses, income, tax credits, etc	Tick this box if the items entered in the box had foreign tax taken off		Partner's share of profits, losses, income, tax credits, etc	Copy figures in boxes 11 to 29 to boxes in the individual's Partnership (short) pages as shown below
• **for an accounting period ended in 2016–17**	▼			
from box 3.83 Profit from a trade or profession	**A**	**11** £	Profit **11** £	Copy this figure to box 8
from box 3.82 Adjustment on change of basis		**11A** £	**11A** £	Copy this figure to box 10
from box 3.84 Loss from a trade or profession	**B**	**12** £	Loss **12** £	Copy this figure to box 8
from box 10.4 Business Premises Renovation Allowance		**12A** £	**12A** £	Copy this figure to box 15
• **for the period 6 April 2016 to 5 April 2017***				
from box 7.9A UK taxed interest and taxed alternative finance receipts		**22** £	**22** £	Copy this figure to box 28
from box 3.97 CIS deductions made by contractors on account of tax		**24** £	**24** £	Copy this figure to box 30
from box 3.98 Other tax taken off trading income		**24A** £	**24A** £	Copy this figure to box 31
from box 7.8A Income Tax taken off		**25** £	**25** £	Copy this figure to box 29
from box 3.117 Partnership charges		**29** £	**29** £	Copy this figure to box 4, 'Other tax reliefs' section on page Ai 2 in your personal tax return

* if you are a 'CT Partnership' see the Partnership Tax Return Guide

SA800 2016 PARTNERSHIP TAX RETURN: PAGE 6

(Adapted from HMRC, 2016)

Task 5

Z plc makes up accounts for a 15 month period to 31 March 2017.

(a) Identify how the company will apportion its property income for the long period of account between the accounting periods. Tick ONE box.

	✓
Any way the company chooses	
On a time basis	
On an accruals basis	
On a receipts basis	

(b) Decide how the company will deal with its capital allowances computations for the long period of account. Tick ONE box.

	✓
One computation for the whole 15 month period prorating the allowances up accordingly	
Two computations; one for 12 months, and one for 3 months prorating the allowances down accordingly	

A company has the following information for the 9 months to 30 June 2016:

- Trading profits are £90,900.
- Dividends received (net) are £13,500.
- The company has no related 51% group companies.

(c) The corporation tax liability for nine months to 30 June 2016 is:

£	

Task 6

Jayden starts in business as a sole trader on 6 April 2016. Her adjusted trading profit for the year to 5 April 2017 is £8,100.

(a) Jayden's Class 2 NICs payable for 2016/17 are:

£		.	

(b) Jayden's Class 4 NICs payable for 2016/17 are:

£		.	

Task 7

You have been instructed by a new client who started trading on 1 May 2016. He is concerned about some important dates when he should contact HM Revenue & Customs. He has never filled in a tax return.

State:

(a) The date when he should inform HM Revenue & Customs that he is chargeable to income tax: (insert dates as xx/xx/xxxx)

(b) The date when his first tax return should be filed, if it is to be filed online:

(c) The date income tax will have to be paid (assuming he has any) for his first year of trading:

Task 8

Zowie made a trading loss of £10,000 in her period of account to 31 March 2017.

Identify whether the following statements are true or false.

	True ✓	False ✓
Zowie can set the loss against her general income in 2016/17.		
Zowie can carry the loss forward against her trading profits in 2017/18.		
Zowie can set the loss against her general income in 2017/18.		
Zowie can set the loss against her general income in 2015/16.		

Task 9

You receive the following email from a client.

From: Charlotte@berkshire.com
To: accountant@advice.com

I am thinking of setting up a limited company and offering my services as a PR consultant through my company.

I am currently employed as a PR Manager but think I may be better off if I work through a company and invoice my employer, as a friend has told me I would pay less tax that way.

I would be grateful if you would send me some more information.

Many thanks

Charlotte

(a) Briefly summarise the IR35 legislation.

(b) Explain whether or not you think the IR35 legislation may affect Charlotte.

Task 10

Treasure Ltd sold 2,500 shares in Williams Ltd for £102,100 in June 2016.

2,000 shares had been bought in November 2001 for £50,000.

In February 2006, Treasure Ltd took up a rights issue of 1 for 2 shares, at £20 per share.

Indexation factors

November 2001 to February 2006	0.119
February 2006 to June 2016	0.345

Using the proforma layout provided, calculate the capital gain arising from the disposal of the shares in Williams Ltd. Clearly show the number of shares, and their value, to carry forward.

Share pool

	No. of shares	Cost £	Indexed cost £

Gain

	£

Task 11

(a) DEF plc bought a factory for use in its trade on 10 December 2010 for £120,000. It sold the factory for £230,000 on 1 May 2016.

Assumed Indexation factors

December 2010 to May 2016 0.142

(i) The gain on disposal of the factory is:

£	

(ii) The dates during which a new asset must be acquired for a rollover relief claim to be made are between: (insert dates as xx/xx/xxxx)

and

(iii) If a new factory is acquired for £200,000, the amount of the gain which can be rolled-over is:

£	

Sami gives a shop which he has used in his trade to his son Troy in August 2016. The shop was acquired for £120,000 and was worth £150,000 at the date of the gift. A claim for gift relief is made.

(b) Identify which of the following statements are correct.

	✓
Troy will acquire the shop at a cost of £120,000.	
Sami will have no chargeable gain on the gift.	
The annual exempt amount is deducted before gift relief.	
Troy will acquire the shop at a cost of £150,000.	

BPP PRACTICE ASSESSMENT 3
BUSINESS TAX

ANSWERS

Business Tax (BSTX)
BPP practice assessment 3

Task 1

(a)

Profit	172,820
Disallowed items added back	
Qualifying charitable donation	5,000
Parking fines paid for a director	160
Depreciation charge	65,230
Donation to a political party	850
Total added back	71,240
Allowed items deducted	
Profit on sale of shares	45,777
Dividends received	40,500
Capital allowances	38,750
Total deducted	125,027
Adjusted trading profits	119,033

(b)

	True ✓	False ✓
Badges of trade have developed mainly through case law.	✓	
If a trader inherits an asset and he sells it shortly afterwards, it will appear likely that he is trading.		✓
If a trader enhances an asset to make it more desirable to a buyer, this is indicative of trading.	✓	

Task 2

(a)

	Total £	Gerry £	Harold £	Iris £
Year ended 31.12.16	27,000	18,000	9,000	0
Year ended 31.12.17	35,000	14,000	14,000	7,000

(b) The taxable trading profit for each partner for 2016/17 is:

Gerry:

£	18,000

Harold:

£	9,000

Iris:

£	1,750

Working:

Gerry and Harold

y/e 31.12.16 current year basis

Iris

First year of trading: actual basis 1 January 2017 to 5 April 2017

3/12 × £7,000

Task 3

	AIA £	FYA £	Main pool £	Car (70%) £	Allowances £
AIA additions					
Plant and machinery	239,750				
Motor van	35,500				
Plant and machinery	8,500				
	283,750				
AIA £200,000 × 15/12 (max)	(250,000)				250,000
	33,750				
Transfer balance to main pool	(33,750)		33,750		
Non-AIA addition					
Car				9,600	
Car		12,500			
FYA @ 100%		(12,500)			12,500
WDA @ 18% × 15/12			(7,594)		7,594
WDA @ 8% × 15/12				(960) × 70%	672
c/f			26,156	8,640	
Allowances					270,766

Note. Both the AIA and the WDA are time apportioned for a long period of account, but not the FYA.

Task 4

Partnership tax adjusted trading profit £(210,000 – 70,000 – 69,710 – 13,200) = £57,090

Page 6

Box 1	01.04.16
Box 2	31.03.17
Box 3	Fishmongers
Box 11	£57,090
Box 6	Fred Fisher
Box 11	£38,060

Task 5

(a)

	✓
Any way the company chooses	
On a time basis	✓
On an accruals basis	
On a receipts basis	

(b)

	✓
One computation for the whole 15 month period prorating the allowances up accordingly	
Two computations; one for 12 months, and one for 3 months prorating the allowances down accordingly	✓

(c) The corporation tax liability for nine months to 30 June 2016 is:

£	18,180

Working:

Dividends are not taxable so TTP = £90,900

£90,900 × 20% = £18,180

Task 6

(a) Jayden's Class 2 NICs payable for 2016/17 are:

£	145	.	60

Working:

(£2.80 × 52)

(b) Jayden's Class 4 NICs payable for 2016/17 are:

£	3	.	60

Working:

(8,100 – 8,060) × 9%.

Task 7

(a) The date when he should inform HM Revenue & Customs that he is chargeable to income tax:

05/10/2017

(b) The date when his first tax return should be filed, if it is to be filed online:

31/01/2018

(c) The date income tax will need to be paid (assuming he has any) for his first year of trading:

31/01/2018

Task 8

	True ✓	False ✓
Zowie can set the loss against her general income in 2016/17.	✓	
Zowie can carry the loss forward against her trading profits in 2017/18.	✓	
Zowie can set the loss against her general income in 2017/18.		✓
Zowie can set the loss against her general income in 2015/16.	✓	

Task 9

(a)

The IR35 legislation exists to prevent Personal Service Companies (PSCs) being used to disguise employment.

It is applied where the relationship between the client and the worker would be deemed to be one of employment, were it not for the existence of the PSC.

The effect of the legislation is for the client's payments to be taxed as employment income on the worker.

(b)

If Charlotte carries on doing the same job for the same company then HMRC are likely to consider her to have an employment relationship, and the legislation would apply to her.

Task 10

Share pool

	No. of shares	Cost £	Indexed cost £
November 2001	2,000	50,000	50,000
Index to February 2006			
£50,000 × 0.119			5,950
Rights issue 1 for 2 @ £20 each	1,000	20,000	20,000
	3,000	70,000	75,950
Index to June 2016			
£75,950 × 0.345			26,203
	3,000	70,000	102,153
Less sale	(2,500)	(58,333)	(85,128)
Carry forward	500	11,667	17,025

Gain

			£
Disposal proceeds			102,100
Less cost			(58,333)
			43,767
Indexation (85,128 – 58,333)			(26,795)
Chargeable gain			16,972

Task 11

(a) **(i)** The gain on disposal of the factory is:

£	88,040

Workings:

	£
Proceeds of sale	230,000
Less cost	(120,000)
	110,000
Less indexation allowance £120,000 × 0.142	(17,040)
Chargeable gain	92,960

(ii) The dates during which a new asset must be acquired for a rollover relief claim to be made are between:

01/05/2015

and

01/05/2019

(iii) If a new factory is acquired for £200,000, the amount of the gain which can be rolled-over is:

£	62,960

Workings:

Gain immediately chargeable £(230,000 – 200,000)	30,000
Gain which can be rolled-over £(92,960 – 30,000)	62,960

(b)

	✓
Troy will acquire the shop at a cost of £120,000.	✓
Sami will have no chargeable gain on the gift.	✓
The annual exempt amount is deducted before gift relief.	
Troy will acquire the shop at a cost of £150,000.	

Troy will acquire the shop at MV less gift relief £(150,000 – 30,000), gift relief of £30,000 leaves Sami with no gain.

Gift relief cannot be restricted to allow Sami to use his annual exempt amount.

BPP PRACTICE ASSESSMENT 4
BUSINESS TAX

Time allowed: 2 hours

Business Tax (BSTX)
BPP practice assessment 4

In the live assessment you will have access to the Tax tables and reference material which have been reproduced at the back of this Question Bank (see page 241–259). Please use them whilst completing this practice assessment so that you are familiar with their content.

Task 1

The statement of profit or loss Jeremy Ltd for the year to 31 March 2017 shows the following information:

	£	£
Gross profit		512,500
Profit on sale of shares		13,550
Dividends received		6,300
Interest income		4,500
		536,850
General expenses (note 1)	210,780	
Motor expenses (note 2)	40,500	
Wages and salaries	110,350	
Administrative expenses	77,230	
Depreciation charge	15,700	
		(454,560)
Profit for the year		82,290

Notes

1 **General expenses**

These include:

	£
Qualifying charitable donation (paid August 2016)	500
Entertaining customers	9,550
Entertaining staff	8,650

2 **Motor expenses**

These include:

	£
Parking fines incurred by director	610
Petrol used by director for private use	6,300
Leasing costs of car for director (CO_2 emissions 180 g/km)	9,300

3 **Capital allowances**

The capital allowances for the year ended 31 March 2017 are £8,750.

Using the proforma layout provided, compute the adjusted trading profit for Jeremy Ltd for the year to 31 March 2017. Fill in all unshaded boxes. Add a 0 (zero) if necessary.

	£	£
Profit for the year per accounts		82,290
	Add	Deduct
Profit on sale of shares		
Dividends received		
Interest income		
Qualifying charitable donation		
Entertaining customers		
Entertaining staff		
Parking fines incurred by director		

Petrol used by director for private use		
Leasing costs of car for director		
Wages and salaries		
Administrative expenses		
Depreciation charge		
Capital allowances		
Total to add/deduct		
Taxable trading profit		

Task 2

Xavier, Yvonne and Zebedee have been in partnership for many years making up accounts to 30 September each year. Under the partnership agreement, Xavier is entitled to a salary of £9,000 a year and the profits are then divided 2:2:1 between the partners respectively.

Xavier retired from the partnership on 31 December 2016. Yvonne and Zebedee carried on the partnership and the partnership agreement was altered so that the profits were then divided 2:1 between Yvonne and Zebedee respectively.

The partnership profits for the year to 30 September 2017 were £209,000.

(a) Using the proforma layout provided, show the division of the partnership profit for the year to 30 September 2017. Fill in all unshaded boxes and add a 0 (zero) if necessary.

	Total £	Xavier £	Yvonne £	Zebedee £
Period to 31/12/2016				
Salary				
Share of profits				
Period to 30/09/2017				
Share of profits				
Total profit for y/e 30/09/2017				

You see from your files that Xavier's share of the partnership profit for the year to 30 September 2016 was £21,000 and that he had overlap profits of £4,500 on commencement.

(b) Xavier's taxable partnership profits for the tax year of cessation are:

£	

Task 3

Codie is in business as a sole trader making up accounts to 31 March each year. You have been asked to complete her capital allowances computation for the year to 31 March 2017. The following information is relevant:

(1) The capital allowance computation showed the following written-down value at 1 April 2016:

	£
Main pool	58,060

(2) During the period 1 April 2016 to 31 March 2017, Codie had the following capital transactions:

Purchases		£
April 2016	Plant and machinery	5,030
May 2016	Plant and machinery	204,250
July 2016	Car (CO_2 emissions 110g/km)	19,320 (80% private use)
Disposals		
January 2017	Plant and machinery	23,900

Compute Codie's capital allowances computation for the year to 31 March 2017.

Task 4

Complete the following extract from the tax return for Byatt Ltd for the year ended 31 March 2016, using the following information:

	£
Revenue	320,000
Trade profits	215,000
Chargeable gain	18,000
Qualifying charitable donation paid	3,000
Trading loss brought forward	(15,000)
Capital loss brought forward	(2,000)

Tax calculation

Turnover

145	Total turnover from trade	£ . 0 0
150	Banks, building societies, insurance companies and other financial concerns – *put an 'X' in this box if you do not have a recognised turnover and have not made an entry in box 145*	☐

Income

155	Trading profits	£ . 0 0
160	Trading losses brought forward claimed against profits	£ . 0 0
165	Net trading profits – *box 155 minus box 160*	£ . 0 0
170	Bank, building society or other interest, and profits from non-trading loan relationships	£ . 0 0
172	Put an 'X' in box 172 if the figure in box 170 is net of carrying back a deficit from a later accounting period	☐
175	Annual payments not otherwise charged to Corporation Tax and from which Income Tax has not been deducted	£ . 0 0

Income *continued*

180	Non-exempt dividends or distributions from non-UK resident companies	£ . 0 0
185	Income from which Income Tax has been deducted	£ . 0 0
190	Income from a property business	£ . 0 0
195	Non-trading gains on intangible fixed assets	£ . 0 0
200	Tonnage Tax profits	£ . 0 0
205	Income not falling under any other heading	£ . 0 0

Chargeable gains

210	Gross chargeable gains	£ . 0 0
215	Allowable losses including losses brought forward	£ . 0 0
220	Net chargeable gains - *box 210 minus box 215*	£ . 0 0

Profits before deductions and reliefs

225	Losses brought forward against certain investment income	£ . 0 0
230	Non-trade deficits on loan relationships (including interest) and derivative contracts (financial instruments) brought forward	£ . 0 0
235	Profits before other deductions and reliefs - *net sum of boxes 165 to 205 and 220 minus sum of boxes 225 and 230*	£ . 0 0

Deductions and reliefs

240	Losses on unquoted shares	£ . 0 0
245	Management expenses	£ . 0 0
250	UK property business losses for this or previous accounting period	£ . 0 0
255	Capital allowances for the purposes of management of the business	£ . 0 0
260	Non-trade deficits for this accounting period from loan relationships and derivative contracts (financial instruments)	£ . 0 0

(Adapted from HMRC, 2016)

Task 5

K Ltd decides to make up accounts for a 15 month period of account to 30 November 2016. Trading profits were £10,000 per month for the first 10 months and £12,000 per month thereafter. It made a capital gain of £10,000 in January 2016 and a capital gain of £20,000 in October 2016.

Identify whether the following statements are true or false.

	True ✓	False ✓
The gain of £10,000 will be dealt with in the accounting period to 31 August 2016 and the gain of £20,000 will be dealt with in the accounting period to 30 November 2016.		
Trading profits will be £124,000 in the accounting period to 31 August 2016 and £36,000 in the accounting period to 30 November 2016.		

Task 6

Abdul is in business as a sole trader. His taxable trading profits for 2016/17 are £56,000, and he receives dividends of £9,000 in July 2016.

The Class 2 NIC liability for 2016/17 is:

£		.	

The Class 4 NIC liability for 2016/17 is:

£		.	

The total NIC liability for 2016/17 is:

£		.	

Task 7

SR plc makes up accounts to 31 October each year. It is not a large company.

The corporation tax liability of SR plc for the year to 31 October 2016 was £24,000 and for the year to 31 October 2017 was £36,000.

(a) How will SR plc pay the corporation tax liability for the year to 31 October 2017?

	✓
Four instalments of £6,000 each due on 14 May 2017, 14 August 2017, 14 November 2017 and 14 February 2018 with a balancing payment of £12,000 due on 14 April 2018	
One payment due on 31 January 2019	
Four instalments of £9,000 each due on 14 May 2017, 14 August 2017, 14 November 2017 and 14 February 2018	
One payment due on 1 August 2018	

(b) Tick the appropriate box for each of the following statements.

	True ✓	False ✓
The maximum penalty for an error in a tax return which is deliberate but not concealed is 75%.		
If an individual submits his 2016/17 tax return online on 13 January 2018, HMRC can start an enquiry at any time before 31 January 2019.		
If a company submits its tax return two months late, the penalty is £100.		

Task 8

Osian makes a trading loss of £5,000 in 2016/17. He has property income of £6,300 in 2016/17. Osian had taxable trading income of £15,000 in 2015/16 and property income of £2,000.

(a) Identify whether the following statements are true or false.

	True ✓	False ✓
Osian can claim to use his loss of 2016/17 against his general income in 2015/16 only, in order to preserve his personal allowance in 2016/17.		
Osian can claim to use his loss of 2016/17 against his trading income in 2015/16 only, in order to preserve his personal allowance in 2016/17.		
Osian must claim to use his loss of 2016/17 against his general income in 2016/17, before being able to carry it back.		

(b) Identify whether the following statements are true or false for a company.

	True ✓	False ✓
When a trading loss is carried back by a company, it is set-off after deducting qualifying charitable donations.		
A company can carry a trade loss back 12 months against total profits and forward 36 months against profits of the same trade.		
A company must set-off trading losses in the current period before carrying back to the previous period.		

Task 9

(a) Which TWO of the following are not fundamental principles of professional ethics?

	✓
Confidentiality	
Professional intellect	
Integrity	
Courtesy and consideration	
Professional competence and due care	

(b) Which of the following actions by a taxpayer would not constitute tax evasion?

	✓
Earning tax free dividends in an ISA	
Deciding not to declare trading income earned	
Failing to notify HMRC of starting to earn rental income	
Claiming capital allowances on a non-existent piece of plant or machinery	

Task 10

Ros bought 2,000 shares in Blueberry Ltd for £10,000 in November 2007.

In March 2009, she received 400 shares in a bonus issue. In May 2011 the company offered a rights issue at 1 share for every 6 held. She accepted this rights issue at £3 per share. She sold 1,800 shares in Blueberry Ltd in July 2016 for £13,500.

Using the proforma layouts provided, show the chargeable gain on sale.

Share pool

	No of shares	Cost £

Gain

	£
Proceeds of sale	
Less allowable cost	
Chargeable gain	

Task 11

Three taxpayers sold similar assets during 2016/17 and each made a capital gain, after deducting their annual exemption (annual exempt amount), of £21,000. In the table below, the total of their other taxable income is shown.

Show the amount of capital gain that would be chargeable under each of the two rates of capital gains tax (CGT). You must enter 0 if your answer is zero.

		Chargeable capital gain £	
Taxpayer	Other income £	10% CGT rate	20% CGT rate
Peter	11,300		
Richard	26,100		
Gemma	66,800		

BPP PRACTICE ASSESSMENT 4
BUSINESS TAX

ANSWERS

Business Tax (BSTX)
BPP practice assessment 4

Task 1

Jeremy Ltd adjusted trading profit for the year ending 31 March 2017

	£	£
Profit for the year per accounts		82,290
	Add	Deduct
Profit on sale of shares	0	13,550
Dividends received	0	6,300
Interest income	0	4,500
Qualifying charitable donation	500	0
Entertaining customers	9,550	0
Entertaining staff	0	0
Parking fines incurred by director	610	0
Petrol used by director for private use	0	0
Leasing costs of car for director (£9,300 × 15%)	1,395	0
Wages and salaries	0	0
Administrative expenses	0	0
Depreciation charge	15,700	0
Capital allowances	0	8,750
Total to add/deduct	27,755	33,100
Taxable trading profit		76,945

Task 2

(a)

	Total £	Xavier £	Yvonne £	Zebedee £
Period to 31/12/2016				
Salary (× 3/12)	2,250	2,250	0	0
Share of profits (2:2:1)	50,000	20,000	20,000	10,000
Period to 30/09/2017				
Share of profits (2:1)	156,750	0	104,500	52,250
Total profit for y/e 30/09/2017	209,000	22,250	124,500	62,250

(b) Xavier's taxable partnership profits for the tax year of cessation are:

£	38,750

Workings:

2016/17	£
Profit for y/e 30 September 2016	21,000
Profit for p/e 31 December 2016	22,250
Less overlap profit	(4,500)
Taxable profit for 2016/17	38,750

Task 3

Year ended 31 March 2017

	AIA £	Main pool £	Car (20% business) £	Allowances £
B/f		58,060		
AIA additions				
April 2016	5,030			
May 2016	204,250			
	209,280			
AIA	(200,000)			200,000
Transfer to main pool		9,280		
Disposals		(23,900)		
Non-AIA addition				
Car			19,320	
		43,440		
WDA @ 18%		(7,819)		7,819
WDA @ 18%			(3,478) × 20%	696
		35,621	15,842	208,515

Task 4

Box 145 £320,000
Box 155 £215,000
Box 160 £15,000
Box 165 £200,000
Box 210 £18,000
Box 215 £2,000
Box 220 £16,000
Box 235 £216,000

Task 5

	True ✓	False ✓
The gain of £10,000 will be dealt with in the accounting period to 31 August 2016 and the gain of £20,000 will be dealt with in the accounting period to 30 November 2016.	✓	
Trading profits will be £124,000 in the accounting period to 31 August 2016 and £36,000 in the accounting period to 30 November 2016.		✓

Trading profits will be £128,000 in the accounting period to 31 August 2016 and £32,000 in the accounting period to 30 November 2016, as they are time apportioned evenly.

Task 6

The Class 2 NIC liability for 2016/17 is:

£	145	.	60

Working:

(£2.80 × 52)

The Class 4 NIC liability for 2016/17 is:

£	3,404	.	60

Working:

£(43,000 – 8,060) × 9% + £(56,000 – 43,000) × 2%

The total NIC liability for 2016/17 is:

£	3,550	.	20

Task 7

(a)

	✓
Four instalments of £6,000 each due on 14 May 2017, 14 August 2017, 14 November 2017 and 14 February 2018 with a balancing payment of £12,000 due on 14 April 2018	
One payment due on 31 January 2019	
Four instalments of £9,000 each due on 14 May 2017, 14 August 2017, 14 November 2017 and 14 February 2018	
One payment due on 1 August 2018	✓

(b)

	True ✓	False ✓
The maximum penalty for an error in a tax return which is deliberate but not concealed is 75%.		✓ (70%)
If an individual submits his 2016/17 tax return online on 13 January 2018, HMRC can start an enquiry at any time before 31 January 2019.		✓ (return submitted by due date: one year from actual filing date)
If a company submits its tax return two months late, the penalty is £100.	✓	

Task 8

(a)

	True ✓	False ✓
Osian can claim to use his loss of 2016/17 against his general income in 2015/16 only, in order to preserve his personal allowance in 2016/17.	✓	
Osian can claim to use his loss of 2016/17 against his trading income in 2015/16 only, in order to preserve his personal allowance in 2016/17.		✓
Osian must claim to use his loss of 2016/17 against his general income in 2016/17, before being able to carry it back.		✓

(b)

	True ✓	False ✓
When a trading loss is carried back by a company, it is set-off after deducting qualifying charitable donations.		✓
A company can carry a trading loss back 12 months against total profits and forward 36 months against profits of the same trade.		✓
A company must set-off trading losses in the current period before carrying back to the previous period.	✓	

When a trading loss is carried back by a company, it is set-off before deducting qualifying charitable donations.

When trade losses are carried forward there is no restriction, they are carried forward indefinitely.

Task 9

(a)

	✓
Confidentiality	
Professional intellect	✓
Integrity	
Courtesy and consideration	✓
Professional competence and due care	

"Professional intellect" and "Professional competence and due care" would be required of a professional accountant but are not of themselves fundamental principles.

(b)

	✓
Earning tax free dividends in an ISA	✓
Deciding not to declare trading income earned	
Failing to notify HMRC of starting to earn rental income	
Claiming capital allowances on a non-existent piece of plant or machinery	

Earning tax free dividends in an ISA is a legitimate way to reduce tax.

Task 10

Share pool

	No. of shares	Cost £
November 2007 Acquisition	2,000	10,000
March 2009 Bonus	400	Nil
	2,400	10,000
May 2011 Rights 1 for 6 @ £3	400	1,200
	2,800	11,200
July 2016 Disposal	(1,800)	(7,200)
c/f	1000	4,000

Gain

	£
Proceeds of sale	13,500
Less allowable cost	(7,200)
Chargeable gain	6,300

Task 11

		Chargeable capital gain £	
Taxpayer	Other income £	10% CGT rate	20% CGT rate
Peter	11,300	20,700	300
Richard	26,100	5,900	15,100
Gemma	66,800	0	21,000

Tax reference material FA 2016

Taxation tables for Business Tax – 2016/17

Note that 'TAXATION DATA 1' and 'TAXATION DATA 2' shown below will be available as pop up windows throughout your live assessment.

TAXATION DATA 1

Capital allowances	
Annual investment allowance	
From 1/6 April 2014	£500,000
From 1 January 2016	£200,000
Plant and machinery writing down allowance	
Long life assets and integral-features	8%
Other assets	18%
Motor cars	
CO_2 emissions up to 75 g/km	100%
CO_2 emissions between 76 and 130 g/km	18%
CO_2 emissions over 130 g/km	8%
Energy efficient and water saving plant	
First year allowance	100%
Capital gains	
Annual exempt amount	£11,100
Standard rate (residential property/other disposals)	18/10%
Higher rate (residential property/other disposals)	28/20%
Entrepreneurs' relief rate	10%
Entrepreneurs' relief limit	£10,000,000
National insurance rates	
Class 2 contributions	£2.80 per week
Small earnings exemption	£5,965 p.a.
Class 4 contributions:	
Main rate	9%
Additional rate	2%
Lower profits limit	£8,060
Upper profits limit	£43,000

Taxation data 2

Corporation tax		
Financial year	2016	2015
All profits and gains	20%	20%

Introduction to business tax

Administration

- Taxation administered by HM Revenue & Customs (HMRC).
- Rules covering tax are contained in statute (law). Law passed every year (Finance Act).
- Decisions reached by the courts interpreting the law are known as case law.
- HMRC also issue guidance – Extra Statutory Concessions and Statements of Practice.

Taxes

- Corporation Tax – paid by companies on both income and capital gains.
- Income Tax – paid by individuals on their income.
- Capital Gains Tax – paid by individuals on their capital gains.

Tax avoidance and tax evasion

- **Tax evasion**

  Any action taken to evade tax by illegal means; this carries a risk of criminal prosecution.

  Examples or tax evasion include failing to declare income and claiming false expenses.

- **Tax avoidance**

  Use of legitimate means to minimise taxpayer's tax liability, for example by investing in a tax-free ISA (Individual Savings Account).

Adjustment of profits – sole traders, partnerships and companies

Pro forma for adjustment of profits

	£	£
Net profit as per accounts		X
Add: Expenses charge in the accounts that are not allowable as trading expenses	X	
		X
		X
Less: Income included in the accounts which is not accessible as trading income	X	
		(X)
Adjusted profit/(loss)		X

Disallowed expenses

- Expenses that fail the remoteness test so not "wholly and exclusively" for trading purposes.
- Fines on the business or fraud by directors/owners.
- Donations to national charities – might be allowed as a charge on income if Gift Aid donations. Political donations are never allowable.
- Capital expenditure eg purchase of equipment included in profit and loss account.
- Depreciation. Capital allowances granted instead.
- Costs of bringing newly acquired second-hand assets to useable condition.
- Legal and professional expenses relating to capital items or breaking the law.
- Customer entertaining. Staff entertaining can be allowable.
- Customer gifts unless gift incorporates business advertising, cost is less than £50 per annum per customer and gift is not food, drink, tobacco or cash vouchers.

Non-assessable income

- Income taxed in any other way, eg interest or property income for individuals.
- Profits on sale of fixed assets.

Unincorporated businesses – trading income

Trading income calculated for each period of account:

	£
Adjusted accounting profit	X
Less: Capital allowances	
Plant and machinery	(X)
Plus: Balancing charges	X
Trading income for the period of account	X

Expenses charged in the accounts which are not allowable as trading expenses

- See Adjustment of profits – sole traders, partnerships and companies
- Transactions with the owner of the business. For eg:
  - Add back salary paid to owner. Salaries paid to family members do not need to be added back.
  - Private expenditure included in accounts.
  - Class 2 National Insurance contributions.
  - Goods taken for own use.

Private use assets

- Private use assets have separate column in Capital Allowance computation.
- Disallow private use % of WDA/AIA/FYA.

Capital allowances – business cessation

- In the cessation period of account, no WDA/AIA/FYA.
- Include additions and disposals as normal. Any asset taken over by owner, treat as a disposal at market value. Balancing adjustment made (balancing charge or balancing allowance).

Sole traders – basis periods

Tax year – 2016/17 tax year runs from 6 April 2016 to 5 April 2017

Basis period rules

- First year – runs from start date of trading to the next 5 April.
- Second year and third year:

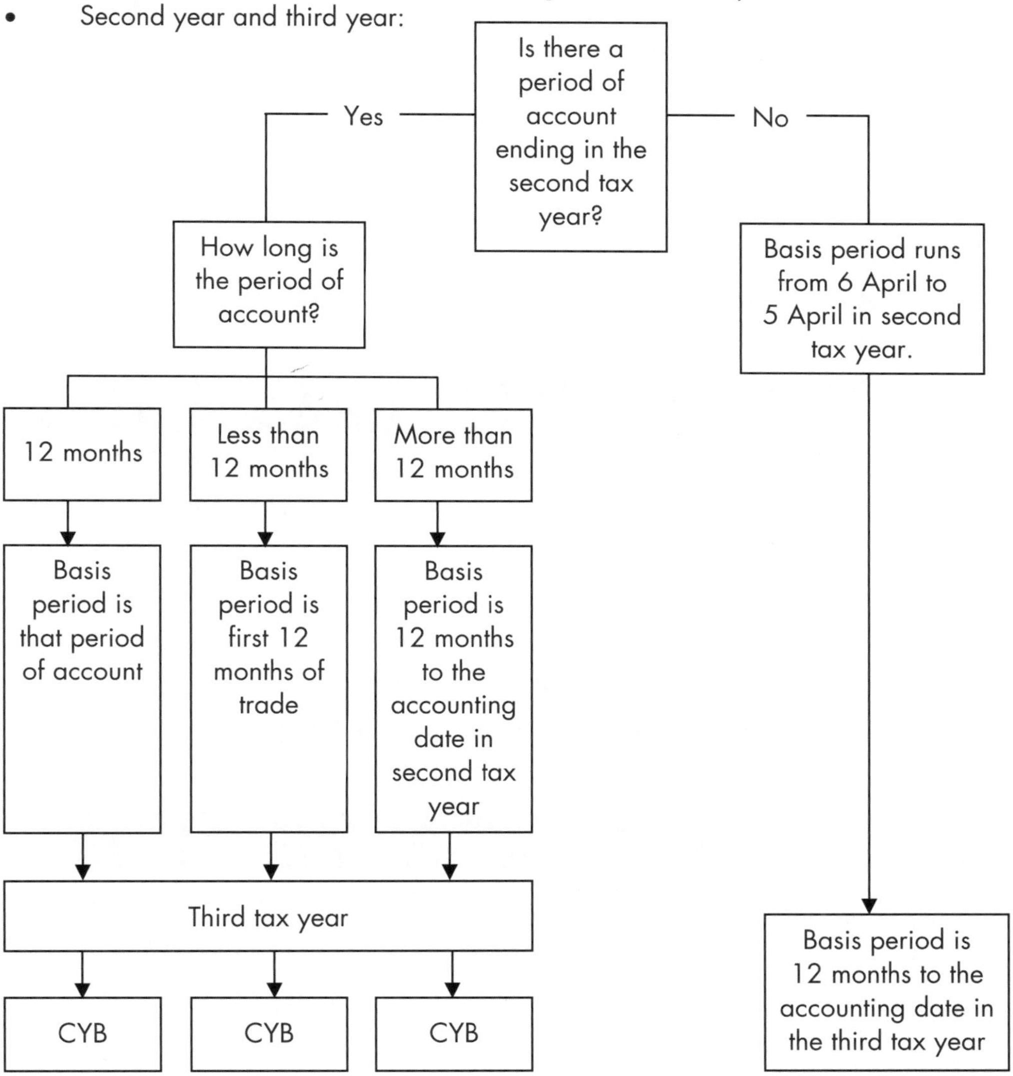

Later years – basis period is the period of account ending in the tax year = Current Year basis (CYB).

Final year – basis period is the period from the end of the basis period for the previous tax year to cessation date.

Overlap profits – opening year rules may lead to profits being taxed twice. Relief is given on cessation of the business.

Sole traders – change of accounting date

For an accounting date change to be recognised for tax purposes the following conditions must be satisfied.

- The first accounts ending on the new date must not exceed 18 months in length.
- The sole trader or partnership must give notice of the change in the tax return by the filing date of the tax return.

Year of change – is the first tax year in which accounts are made up to the new date.

Relevant period – is the time to the new accounting date from the end of the previous basis period.

Example 1 – relevant period is less than 12 months

Jasmin changes her accounting date as follows:

Accounts	Year	Basis period
Year to 31 December 2014	2014/15	11/1/14 to 31/12/14
9 months to 30 September 2015	2015/16	1/10/14 to 30/9/15
Year to 30 September 2016	2016/17	1/10/15 to 30/9/16

Year of change – 2015/16

Relevant period – 9 months to 30 September 2015

Example 2 – relevant period is greater than 12 months

Vaughan changes his accounting date as follows:

Accounts	Year	Basis period
Year to 31 December 2014	2014/15	11/1/14 to 31/12/14
15 months to 31 March 2016	2015/16	1/1/15 to 31/3/16
Year to 31 March 2017	2016/17	1/4/16 to 31/3/17

Year of change – 2015/16

Relevant period – 15 months to 31 March 2016

The rules for determining basis periods on a change of accounting date are complex. Significant examples of changes in accounting dates include:

- After the third year of trading
- With accounts of 18 months or less
- Not straddling a tax year.

Capital allowances on plant and machinery

Layout of capital allowances on plant and machinery computation (see Taxation Tables for rates)

	First Year Allowance (FYA) £	Annual Investment Allowance (AIA) £	General pool £	Special rate pool £	Short Life Asset SLA £	Total allowances £
WDV b/f			X	X	X	
Additions	X	X	X			
Disposals	X		(X)		(X)	
	X	X	X	X	X	
Balancing allowance/ balancing charge (BA/BC)					X/(X)	X/(X)
					Nil	
AIA/FYA	(X)	(X)				X
Writing down allowance @ 18% p.a.			(X)			X
Writing down allowance @ 8% p.a.				(X)		X
WDV c/f	Nil	Nil	X	X		
Total allowances						X

- Plant – defined by 'function/setting' distinction and case law.
- AIA – 100% allowance for expenditure (other than cars) in 12 month period (pro-rata). Expenditure in excess of AIA qualifies for writing down allowance (WDA).
- Full WDA for the period is given regardless of date of purchase of item. WDA is scaled for periods other than 12 months.
- FYA – 100% allowance given on purchase of environmentally friendly cars and energy saving/water efficient plant. FYA is not scaled for short accounting periods.

- If the written down value (WDV) on the general pool (= WDV b/f + additions – disposals) is £1,000 or less then pool is written off as small pools annual writing down allowance.
- Short life assets (SLA) – de-pool asset if life expected to be than eight years. Not available for cars.

Partnerships

- Each partner is taxed like a sole trader on their share of the partnership profits.
- First step is to share accounting profits between partners:
  - Allocate the correct salaries and interest on capital for the period to each partner.
  - Divide the remaining profit for each set of accounts between the partners based upon the profit sharing arrangement.
  - You may need to split the period if there is a change such as a partner joining or leaving.
- Opening year and cessation rules apply to partners individually when they join or leave the partnership.
- Allocate the profit for each partner to the correct tax year using basis period rules.
- Basis periods for continuing partners are unaffected by joiners or leavers.
- Each partner enters their share of profits for a tax year in the partnership pages of their own tax return.

Trading losses for sole traders and partners

- A loss is computed in the same way as a profit, making the same adjustments to the net profit as per the accounts and deducting capital allowances.

Set off of trading loss against total income

- Set off loss against total income of the preceding tax year and/or the tax year of loss, eg loss in 2016/17 set off against total income in 2015/16 and/or 2016/17.
- Cannot restrict loss to preserve use of personal allowance so personal allowance may be wasted.
- For 2016/17 loss claim needed by 31 January 2019.

Carry forward of trading losses

- If any loss remains unrelieved after current year and carry back claim has been made, or no such claims are made, then carry forward the loss against first available profits of the same trade.

Choice of loss relief – consider the following:

- Utilise loss in the tax year in which income is taxed at a higher rate.
- Possible wastage of personal allowance.
- Review the projected future profits to ensure the loss can be utilised.
- If cash flow is important, a loss carry back claim may result in a tax refund being paid to the company.

Payment and administration – sole traders and partners

The return must be filed by:

- 31 October following the end of the tax year if filing a paper return.
- 31 January following the end of the tax year if filing online.

Late filing	Late payment	Penalty
Miss filing deadline		£100
	30 days late	5% of tax due, or £300 if greater
3 months late		Daily penalty if £10 per day for up to 90 days (max £900)
6 months late		5% of tax due, or £300 if greater
	6 months late	5% of tax outstanding at that date
12 months late		5%, or £300 if greater
	12 months late	5% of tax outstanding at that date
12 months and information deliberately withheld		Based on behaviour: • Deliberate and concealed withholding 100% of tax due; or £300 if greater • Deliberate but not concealed 70% of tax due, or £300 if greater Reductions of up to half of the above %'s apply for cooperation with investigation

Disclosure and errors

- Taxpayer must notify HMRC by 5 October following end of the tax year if a tax return is needed.
- Taxpayer can amend a tax return within 12 months of filing date or make an error or mistake claim within three years of the filing date.

Payments on account (POA)

- Due 31 January (in tax year) and 31 July (after tax year end). Each instalment is 50% of the previous year's tax and Class 4 NIC liability.
- Balancing payment made 31 January after tax year end.
- No POA due if last year's tax and Class 4 National Insurance contribution (NIC) liability less than £1,000 or greater than 80% if last year's liability was deducted at source.
- Can reduce POA if this year's liability expected to be less than last year's. Penalties will be charged if a deliberate incorrect claim is made.
- Capital gains tax (CGT) liability is paid 31 January following the tax year end. No POA needed for CGT.

Interest on tax paid late/overpaid tax

- Interest charged daily on late payment.

Enquiries and other penalties

- HMRC must notify individual of enquiry within 12 months of submission of return.
- Basis of enquiry – random or HMRC believe income/expenses misstated.
- Penalty for failure to produce enquiry documents = £50 + £30 per day.
- Penalty for failure to keep proper records is up to £3,000. Records must be kept for five years after the filing date for the relevant tax year.

Penalties for incorrect returns are:

Type of behaviour	Maximum	Unprompted (min)	Prompted (min)
Genuine mistake, despite taking reasonable care	0%	0%	0%
Careless error and inaccuracy due to failure to take reasonable care	30%	0%	15%
Deliberate error but not concealed	70%	20%	35%
Deliberate error and concealed	100%	30%	50%

National insurance contributions

- Self-employed individuals pay Class 2 and Class 4 contributions.
- Class 4 contributions are 9% on profits between the lower and upper limits, then 2% on profits above the upper limit.
- Percentage and limits are provided in the Taxation Tables.

An outline of corporate tax

- Companies pay corporation tax on their profits for each accounting period.
- There is one rate of corporation tax set each financial year.
- Profits = income + gains – charges
- Accounting periods are usually 12 months long but can be shorter.
- If a company's accounts are longer than 12 months, the first 12 months will be one accounting period and the remainder a second accounting period.
- All UK property income is pooled as a single source of income and taxed on a accruals basis.

- Borrowing or lending money by a company is a loan relationship.
- Trading loan relationships are part of trading income.
- Non-trading loan relationships (NTL-R) are pooled to give NTL-R credits or deficits.
- Gift Aid Donations are charges on income.
- Associated companies – a company is associated with another if one company controls the other or they are both controlled by the same 'person'.

The calculation of total profits and corporation tax payable

ABC Ltd

Corporation tax computation for the year period ended DD/MM/20XX

	£
Trading Income – accruals basis	X
Interest Income – accruals basis	X
Property Income – accruals basis	X
Chargeable gains	X
	X
Less charges on income – Gift Aid donations	(X)
Total profits	X
Corporation tax payable – total profits × corporation tax rate	X

Key points

- Trading income is adjusted from net profit per company accounts less capital allowances.
- All income in computation to be gross.
- Some income may need to be grossed up. Companies receive interest gross.
- Virtually all interest receivable is taxed as interest income.

Dividends payable by a company are not an allowable expense.

- UK dividends receivable by a company are not taxable.
- Net-off current year capital losses against current year capital gains. If there is a net capital loss carry it forward.
- See Taxation tables for corporation tax rates.

Non 31 March year ends

- For example – year ended 31 December 2016. 3 months of period falls in financial year 2015 (FY15) and 9 months in FY16.
- Apportion Total Profits to FY. Apply correct rate for FY.

Long periods of account

- Will consist of two accounting periods = first 12 months and remainder of period.
- Split profits as follows:
  - Adjusted trading profit and property income – time apportion.
  - Capital allowances – separate computations for each CAP.
  - Interest income – accruals basis.
  - Chargeable gains – according to date of disposal.
  - Charges on income – according to date paid.

Corporate tax – losses

- Can elect to set trading losses against current accounting period total profits. Gift aid donations (charges) will remain unrelieved.
- If the above election is made, can also carry back trading loss to set against total profits within the previous 12 months.
- Trading losses are automatically carried forward to set against the first available profits of the same trade if not utilised by the above two claims.
- If there is a choice of loss relief, firstly consider the rate of loss relief then the timing of relief.
- Set out the use of the losses in a loss memorandum.

Corporation tax – payment and administration

Payment date

- Small companies (annual profits less than £1.5 million): 9 months + 1 day after end of the accounting period (CAP).
- Large companies (annual profits greater than £1.5 million) must estimate year's tax liability and pay 25% of the years liability:
  - 6 months and 14 days after start of CAP
  - 9 months and 14 days after start of CAP
  - 14 days after end of CAP
  - 3 months and 14 days after end of CAP
- Estimate must be revised for each quarter. Penalties may be charged if company deliberately fails to pay sufficient instalments.
- No instalments due for first year company is large unless profits are greater than £10 million.
- Associated companies share the annual profit limit of £1.5 million equally.

Interest on late payments

- Interest charged daily on late payment Overpayment of tax receives interest from HMRC. Interest is taxable/tax allowable as interest income.

Filing the return

- Filed on the later of 12 months after end of CAP or 3 months after the notice to deliver a tax return has been issued.
- Late filing penalties are: less than 3 months late: £100; greater than 3 months late: £200: greater than 6 months late: 10% of tax due per return: greater than 12 months late 20% of tax due per return.
- Company must notify HMRC it is within scope of corporation tax within 3 months of starting to trade.
- Company can amend return within 12 months of the filing date.

Enquiries and other penalties

- HMRC must notify company of enquiry within 12 months of submission of return.
- Basis of enquiry – random or HMRC believe income/expenses misstated.
- Penalty for failure to produce enquiry documents: £50 + £30 per day.
- Penalty for failure to keep proper records is up to £3,000. Records must be retained for six years after the end of the relevant accounting period.
- Penalties for incorrect returns are the same as for sole-traders and partners – see sole traders and partners link.

Current tax reliefs and other tax issues

Research and Development (R&D) tax credits for small and medium sized companies

A small or medium sized enterprise (SME) is a company with less than 500 employees with either:

- An annual turnover under €100 million; or
- A balance sheet under €86 million.

The SME tax relief scheme

From 1 April 2015, the tax relief on allowable R&D costs is 230%.

R&D tax credits

If a company makes a loss, it can choose to receive R&D tax credits instead of carrying forward a loss. The amount of tax credit is limited to the total of PAYE and National Insurance contribution liabilities of the company.

Costs that qualify for R&D tax relief

To qualify as R&D, any activity must contribute directly to seeking an advance in science or technology or must be a qualifying indirect activity.

Intermediaries (IR35) legislation

IR35 legislation prevents personal service companies (PSC) being used to disguise permanent employment.

The rules apply where the relationship between the worker and the client, would be considered to be an employment relationship if the existence of the PSC was ignored.

If the rules apply, a deemed employment income tax charge is charged on the PSC.

The deemed employment income tax charge is calculated based upon the actual payments made to the PSC by the client.

Introduction to chargeable gains

- Individual pays capital gains tax (CGT) on net chargeable gains in a tax year.
- For companies, chargeable gains are included as income in calculating total profits.
- Individuals receive an annual exempt amount from CGT – for 2016/17 this is £11,100.
- Gains/losses arise when a chargeable person makes a chargeable disposal of a chargeable asset.
- Chargeable person – individual or company.
- Chargeable disposal – sale, gift or loss/destruction of the whole or part of an asset. Exempt disposals – on death and gifts to approved charities.
- Chargeable asset – all assets unless exempt. Exempt assets are motor cars and some chattels.

Calculation of capital gains tax

Net chargeable gains – total gains in the tax year after netting off any current year or brought forward losses and the annual exempt amount.

Annual exempt amount (AE)

- For individuals only.
- AE cannot be carried forward or carried back.
- Current year losses must be netted off against current year gains before AE. This means AE can be wasted.
- Brought forward capital losses are set off against current year gains after AE so AE is not wasted.

Calculation of gains and losses for individuals

Proforma cornputation

	£	£
Consideration received		X
Less: Incidental costs of sale		X
Net sale proceeds		NSP
Less: Allowable expenditure		X
Acquisition costs	X	X
Incidental costs of acquisition	X	(X)
Enhancement expenditure	X	
		(Cost)
Gain/(Loss)		X/(X)

- Consideration received is usually sales proceeds, but market value will be used instead of actual consideration where the transaction is a gift or between connected persons.
- An individual is connected with their spouse, lineal relatives (and their spouses) and spouse's relatives (and their spouses).
- Husband and wife/civil partner transfers – nil gain nil loss. Tax planning opportunity.

Part disposals – the cost allocated to the disposal = Cost × (A/(A+B))

A = consideration received on part disposal
B = market value of the remainder of the asset
Chattels – tangible moveable object. Two types:

- Wasting – expected life of 50 years or less (eg racehorse or boat). CGT exempt.
- Non-wasting – expected life greater than 50 years (eg antiques or jewellery).

CGT, £6,000 rule

Buy / Sell	£6,000 or less	More than £6,000
Less than £6,000	Exempt	Allowable loss but proceeds are deemed = £6,000
More than £6,000	Normal calculation of the gain, then compare with 5/3 (gross proceeds – £6,000) – take the lower gain	Chargeable in full

Shares and securities – disposals by individuals

CGT on shares and securities

Disposal of shares and securities are subject to CGT except for listed government securities (gilt-edged securities or 'gilts'), qualifying corporate bonds (eg company loan notes/debentures) and shares held in an Individual Savings Account (ISA).

The identification rules

Used to determine which shares have been sold and what acquisition cost can be deducted from the sale proceeds (eg match the disposal and acquisition).

Disposals are matched:

- Firstly, with acquisitions on the same day as the day of disposal.
- Secondly, with acquisitions made in the 30 days following the date of disposal (FIFO basis).
- Thirdly, with shares from the share pool.

The share pool

- The share pool contains all shares acquired prior to the disposal date.
- Each acquisition is not kept separately, but is 'pooled' together with other acquisitions and a running total kept of the number of shares and the cost of those shares.
- When a disposal from the pool is made, the appropriate number of shares are taken from the pool along with the average cost of those shares.
- The gain on disposal is then calculated.

Bonus issues and rights issues

- Bonus issue – no adjustment to cost needed.
- Rights issue – adjustment to cost needed.

Chargeable gains – reliefs available to individuals

Replacement of business assets (rollover) relief – when a qualifying business asset is sold at a gain, taxpayer can defer gain by reinvesting proceeds in a qualifying replacement asset.

- Deferred gain is deducted from the cost of the replacement asset so gain crystallises when the replacement asset is sold.
- Qualifying assets (original and replacement) – must be used in a trade by the vendor and be land and buildings, fixed plant and machinery or goodwill.
- Qualifying time period – replacement asset must be purchased between one year before and three years after the sale of the original asset.
- Partial reinvestment – only some of the sales proceeds reinvested then the gain taxable is the lower of the full gain and the proceeds not reinvested.

Gift relief (holdover relief) – donee takes over asset at donor's base cost ie the gain is given away along with the asset.

- Qualifying assets – trade assets of donor or shares in any unquoted trading company or personal trading company (individual owns at least 5% of company).

Entrepreneurs' relief – gain taxable at 10% capital gains tax rate.

- The £10 million limit is a lifetime limit which is reduced each time a claim for the relief is made.
- For 2016/17 claim must be made by 31 January 2019.
- Qualifying business disposals (assets must be owned for at least 12 months prior to sale).
  - The whole or part of a business carried on by the individual (alone or in partnership).
  - Assets of the individual's or partnership's trading business that has now ceased.
  - Shares in the individual's 'personal trading company'. Individual must have owned the shares and been an employee of the company for 12 months prior to sale.
- From 17 March 2016, newly issued shares in unlisted trading companies purchased on or after 17 March 2016 by external investors qualify for entrepreneurs' relief provided they are continually held for a minimum of three years from 6 April 2016.

Calculation of gains and losses for companies

Proforma computation

	£	£
Consideration received		X
Less: Incidental costs of sale		X
Net sale proceeds		NSP
Less: Allowable expenditure	X	
Acquisition costs + [indexation factor × expenditure]	X	
Incidental costs of acquisition	X	
Enhancement expenditure	X	
Indexation allowance	X	
		(Cost)
Chargeable gain		Gain

- Indexation allowance is not available where there is an unindexed loss, nor can it turn an unindexed gain into an indexed loss.
- Note that companies do not get an annual exempt amount.
- Losses relieved in order – current year first followed by losses brought forward.

Only relief available to companies is rollover relief:

- Rollover relief is a deferral relief – see [Chargeable gains – reliefs available to individuals] for main rollover relief rules.
- Key differences applying for companies:
  - Indexation is given on disposal of the original asset
  - Goodwill is not a qualifying asset for companies.
  - Gain deferred is the indexed gain.
  - On disposal of the replacement asset, indexation is calculated on the base cost not actual cost.

Shares and securities – disposals by companies

The identification rules – a disposal of shares is matched:

- Firstly, with same-day transactions
- Secondly, with transactions in the previous nine days (FIFO). No indexation allowance is available
- Thirdly, with shares from the 1985 pool (shares bought from 1 April 1982 onwards).

1985 pool – pro forma working

	No. of shares	Cost £	Indexed cost £
Purchase	X	X	X
Index to next operative event			X
			X
Operative event (purchase)	X	X	X
	X	X	X
Index to next operative event	X		X
			X
Operative event (sale)	(X)	(X)	(X)A
Pool carried forward	X	X	X

Operative event = purchase, sale, rights issue. Bonus issue is not an operative event.

Computation

	£
Proceeds	X
Less indexed cost (A from pool)	(X)
Indexed gain	X

The badges of trade

Six badges of trade:

- Subject matter
- Ownership
- Frequency of transactions
- Improvement expenditure
- Reason for sale
- Motive for profit

Duties and responsibilities of a tax adviser

- Maintain client confidentiality at all times.
- AAT members must adopt an ethical approach and maintain an objective outlook.
- Give timely and constructive advice to clients.
- Honest and professional conduct with HMRC
- A tax advisor is liable to a £3,000 penalty if they assist in making an incorrect return.

Notes

Notes

Notes

Notes